*Darla Sue Dollman has been writing for Decoded Everything, a 501(c)(3) nonprofit organization dedicated to expertise and insightful information, for several years. She has a heaping helping of both expertise in a wide variety of topics, and a unique insight into those topics—and a truly wonderful ability to express both in the written word. Darla's writing is pure gold.*

—Victoria Nicks, CEO, Decoded Everything

*Darla Dollman is one of those incredibly unique storytellers who has the ability to pull you into a story to the point that you never want to leave. She has always conducted impeccable research which always includes a personal and loving touch. She is simply one of the best writers I have ever known in my life.*

—John Grasson ECV (E Clampus Vitus), editor/publisher, Dezert Magazine

# COLORADO'S DEADLIEST FLOODS

DARLA SUE DOLLMAN

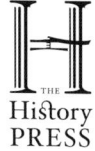

Published by The History Press
Charleston, SC
www.historypress.net

Copyright © 2017 by Darla Sue Dollman
All rights reserved

*Front cover*: Courtesy of Pikes Peak Library District, Stewarts Commercial Photographers Collection.
*Back cover, top*: Courtesy of Pikes Peak Library District, Margaretta M. Boas Photograph Collection; *bottom*: Photo by Steve Zumwalt, FEMA.

First published 2017

Manufactured in the United States

ISBN 9781467137102

Library of Congress Control Number: 2017940946

*Notice*: The information in this book is true and complete to the best of our knowledge. It is offered without guarantee on the part of the author or The History Press. The author and The History Press disclaim all liability in connection with the use of this book.

All rights reserved. No part of this book may be reproduced or transmitted in any form whatsoever without prior written permission from the publisher except in the case of brief quotations embodied in critical articles and reviews.

*This book is dedicated to my children and grandchildren.
Thank you for your love.*

# CONTENTS

Acknowledgements 9
Preface 11
Introduction 17

1. Denver, Gone in a Flash: The Great Flood of 1864 23
2. The Growl of the Big Bear: The Bear Creek Basin Floods
   of 1896 and a History of Floods in the Bear Creek Basin 35
3. Terror in the Night: The Eden Train Wreck of 1904 45
4. Catastrophe at Cherry Creek: The Denver Flood of 1912 55
5. Heroes on the Telephone: The Pueblo Flood of 1921 61
6. The 1933 Castlewood Dam Disaster:
   Telephone Operators Save Lives When Denver Floods 73
7. Miracles and Tragedies: The Monument Creek
   and Kiowa Creek Floods of 1935 83
8. The 1965 Colorado Floods: Catastrophic Flooding
   in the South Platte and Arkansas River Basins 93
9. The Big Thompson Canyon Flood:
   National Celebration Turned Tragedy in 1976 103
10. The Lawn Lake Dam Disaster of 1982 in Estes Park
    and Colorado's Dams 123
11. The Spring Creek Flood of 1997: The Night the Kitten Roared 131
12. Mass Evacuations: The 2013 Colorado Floods 143

Glossary 163
Bibliography 167
About the Author 173

# ACKNOWLEDGEMENTS

I would like to thank my editor, Artie Crisp, for his never-ending patience, knowledge and wisdom. I couldn't have done it without you.

I would also like to thank my family, particularly my grandchildren. Thank you, Layla Marie for supporting and encouraging me and for making me feel special. Thank you, Elijah Louis for inspiring me and sharing your fascination and knowledge of the weather. Thank you, Keller Elway for never forgetting me even when we're far apart. Thank you, Timothy Jack for your hugs. Thank you, Joshuah Peyton for your smiles.

Thank you, Victoria Nicks for your compassion and kindness; for never giving up on me and always treating me as your equal.

Thank you to the many witnesses to the terrible, catastrophic floods in Colorado who shared their stories in this book. Thank you to CarolJoy Collins. You will always be a survivor.

Thank you, Joshuah Agnew and Michelle Levine for sharing your childhood memories of the Spring Creek Flood. Thank you Rusty Golden for jumping into the water to help save others during the flood.

I would like to say a special thank-you to the people of the Big Thompson Canyon, who are keeping the memories of the victims of the Big Thompson Flood sacred. Thank you, Barb Anderson, secretary of the Big Thompson Flood Memorial, for telling your story of the terrible night in the canyon and for sharing your advice, as well as for sharing your heartfelt poetry with the readers. Thank you, Mary Myers for sharing your research, photos and memories. Thank you Fred Bogard, David Grant and Cindi Hendrix for sharing your memories. Thank you,

## Acknowledgements

Stephen Gillette, for sharing your story and helping the people of Estes Park. You are a true hero.

Thank you Ulugbek Khudoynazarov for sharing your memories of the 2013 flooding in Estes Park and for your photographs, as well. Thank you Randy Kady for sharing your memories of the flooding in Loveland during the Colorado Floods of 2013. Thank you Ida Suppress for sharing your painful story of loss and recovery.

It is difficult to thank the many rescue workers involved in these floods. So many people tried to save their neighbors and friends. Others helped in equally important ways, by locating survivors, notifying family members and talking on the phone for days to take and pass on messages. Neighbors brought food, blankets and clothing to survivors. Sergeant Willis Hugh Purdy of the Colorado State Patrol and Officer Michael Owen Conley of the Estes Park Police Department sacrificed their lives attempting to warn residents and tourists to leave the canyon during the Big Thompson Flood, and words of thanks seem hardly enough for such sacrifice. Thank you, former Larimer County sheriff Robert Watson, Colorado state trooper William Miller and the hundreds of officers and National Guardsmen who responded to the call and made a valiant effort to rescue survivors. We will never forget you.

I wish to thank the soldiers who drove their horses into the floodwaters to save the women and children of Denver in the flood of 1864. Then there is the mysterious person who called residents of Denver in 1912 to tell them a flood was coming. Telephone workers stood in freezing water in 1921, calling residents to warn them that the flood was coming their way. The unnamed but never forgotten Douglas County sheriff notified workers at the Sullivan Telephone Exchange that the Castlewood Dam had burst and that everyone and everything for thirty-five miles, from Franktown to Denver, was in the path of a billion gallons of floodwater. Telephone operators worked desperately to pass that message on to everyone they could reach.

The forecasters, meteorologists, dispatchers, ambulance drivers, emergency responders, helicopter pilots, police officers and employees of the sheriff's department and the National Guard—the list of volunteers involved in flood rescue is astounding. Some names are lost to history, and some of these heroes lost their lives, but their acts of heroism set an example that will inspire the people of Colorado for generations to come.

# PREFACE

*It has been said time heals all wounds. I do not agree. The wounds remain.
In time, the mind protecting its sanity covers them with scar tissue
and the pain lessens, but it's never gone.*
—Rose Kennedy

I have always had a fascination with the weather and a deep fear of natural disasters. Through my studies of the weather, I learned of the great loss experienced by many young parents who were unable to protect their children from the overwhelming power of nature. I was obsessed with protecting my own children, with knowing where they were and who they were with so I could call and warn them in the case of emergency. It really isn't such a bad thing when you think about it—it's not obsessive, it's protective. Through the years, though, I realized that no matter how hard we try, we cannot protect our loved ones from the dangerous forces of nature.

Nevertheless, I tried. My children and their friends called me "Doppler Mom." When storm clouds gathered outside and the phone began to ring, they knew it was me.

## A LIFETIME OF STORMY WEATHER

I've had so many experiences with bad weather in my lifetime, from floods to blizzards to ice storms. But it was only when I started writing this book that I realized how deeply I respect and fear nature's power.

# Preface

I decided I wanted to be a writer when I was eight years old. I was much younger when I decided to study the weather, a logical choice for someone raised in the American Southwest. Since my childhood, I have experienced nearly every form of severe weather, except for a tropical cyclone. Many of these experiences came in the form of flash floods in Colorado.

When I was a child, my family lived in Englewood. It was still a small town and separate from the great metropolis of Denver, which today could be said to include Littleton, Englewood, Lakewood, Aurora and everything in between. My first memory of a "flood" came on a spring afternoon. It was raining that day, the type of event people referred to as raining buckets. The water poured thick and fast down the windows and blurred our view of the street.

It was dark as dusk, but I could still see the road in the blinding flashes of lightning that illuminated two rivers flowing down toward our house. The rivers were actually water in the gutters, but they quickly joined into one mass of flowing water stretching from one sidewalk across to the other. It wouldn't be the first time I saw this happen in a Colorado storm. I was frightened and cried with my two sisters as we stared out the window until I heard my mother's voice declare "Enough drama for one day" as she closed the curtains to calm us down.

In spite of my fear, I did notice the threat in our situation. Our house was positioned at the base of two slopes in the road, allowing rainwater to flow in two directions directly onto our property, creating our own personal flood. The situation fascinated me; it became even more fascinating when my mother opened the door to the basement storage room. My sisters and I huddled together, watching as the dark, muddy water filled with floating boxes of clothes and holiday decorations slowly crept up to the first step, then the second, then the third, like some terrible beast in a horror film creeping toward children trembling in the dark.

Eventually, the rain stopped. To me, however, the situation was even more captivating as the water continued to flow into the basement until it reached the top stair. It mysteriously stopped before it could cause any damage to the main floor. The storm seemed alive, making intelligent decisions as to where the water would flow and stop.

This belief of intelligent behavior in storms stayed with me throughout my childhood. I had a difficult childhood (as most people do) and understood at a young age why people compare life to the weather. As a young adult, I understood that storms, like the problems in our lives, do not always stop before creating serious damage. Sometimes, they continue on, leaving a path of destruction that lasts for years—even a lifetime.

# Preface

## A LIFETIME OF NATURAL DISASTERS

The year was 1976. I was a teenager, a fledgling journalist and writer, obsessed with watching the daily newscast and recording the history of Littleton, my hometown, when the most devastating flood in Colorado history, the Big Thompson River Flood, exploded down the canyon and crashed into the city of Loveland with such force that it sent ten-foot chunks of asphalt flying into the air. The water then spread throughout the flatlands, carrying the remains of houses and buildings, trucks and cars and, tragically, 145 residents and tourists who were unable to escape the storm in the dark.

The victims had little or no warning before the floodwaters slammed into their homes. Those who did receive warning were trapped in their vehicles as they tried to escape, screaming for help that would never come. This is what I remember—the stories. The fear in the voices of survivors as they spoke with reporters on the news. I remember seeing a dark cloud over the mountains and believing that it was a debris cloud from the flood. I now believe it was the storm itself. I remember the sound of a grieving mother's voice as she said goodbye to her child who disappeared in the waters.

Most of all, I remember the anger, frustration and shock I felt when I learned that many of the victims could have survived with advance warning. There had been advance knowledge of the storm, of the potential for flooding, of the coming disaster—but not a word was passed on to the people who needed it, those living and camping in the canyon, until it was too late.

## SPRING CREEK DISASTER

I graduated from Colorado State University in 1993. My thesis was bound and archived in the university library. As a former library employee, I was aware that the university was working on an extensive remodel of the campus library and that most of the library's collection was in the basement. In 1997, my family lived in a large house on the opposite side of College Avenue from the university campus.

I've read studies that claim that when someone witnesses a traumatic event, their recollection of facts begins to change within fifteen minutes as their mind adds details it believes should have been there or could have been there based on past experiences. Perhaps this is what happened to me on that day in 1997. It seems impossible now when I imagine the flow of water moving thick as syrup down the window glass, but that is how I've remembered these storms since childhood. I remember the river of water rushing down the streets. I remember cars floating past my house. But I remember no warning. I remember the television screen turning black, a series of high-pitched beeps and then a woman's voice saying, "If you are trying to call 911 we are aware that there is an emergency and we will get to you as soon as we can." It is difficult to believe that this was all we were told, but that's what I remember of that night in Fort Collins in 1997—a woman's frantic voice.

My heart was racing so fast that I thought it would explode. It was raining, and the street in front of my house filled with water within minutes. The water was so high that it covered the lawns and crept up the stairs to the porches. There was only one body of water between me and my teenage son, who was at the home of a friend. It was called Spring Creek. Did the creek flood? I didn't know! We lived a block away from the train tracks. Did a train overturn? What was the emergency and why wouldn't they tell us? In fact, all of these things were occurring at that time—flooding, a train derailed, trailer homes floating down the river. I don't think I took a breath until I saw my car floating down the street with my son at the wheel, guiding it into the driveway.

## FLASH FLOODS HAPPEN EVERYWHERE IN THE UNITED STATES

I spent a few years living in "Flash Flood Alley" in the Texas Hill Country. Trying to survive in this place without losing your home and possessions is an education in itself. My husband and I put a contract on a house near Marble Falls, Texas. We were driving back to Colorado to start our move when one of our children called to confirm the location of our new home, then sadly reported, "I believe that city may be under water." Indeed, the city of Marble Falls was experiencing a massive flood in 2007.

We moved to New Mexico in 2011. Two years later, in September 2013, I awoke to the news that the Big Thompson Canyon was once again flooding. One of my children drove through the canyon every day to her job in Estes Park. I panicked when I saw the broken asphalt on the news and the pictures of trucks and cars falling into the water. My heart pounded in my chest until that moment when I heard her voice on the phone telling me she was safe.

# Preface

The news story quickly changed as the minor flood in Big Thompson Canyon became the floods of 2013, one of the most expensive disasters in the history of Colorado. Aerial photos appeared to show the entire state under water when, in fact, the flooding spread from Colorado Spring to the city of Fort Collins—two hundred miles and seventeen counties. I wanted to drive back to Colorado to help my family and friends, but New Mexico experienced catastrophic floods at the same time. I couldn't help my family. It was too dangerous.

Danger. From my first childhood experience with flooding, I have always understood that there is nothing humans can do to predict or control natural disasters. We will always be at the mercy of the weather. The more I explored the history of floods in Colorado and read about the stories of the people who died—and the ones who survived—the more difficult it became to write this book. Deep inside my heart I felt the pain of the man who learned that his daughters were swept away in the floodwaters of the 1896 Bear Creek disaster. When I read her story, I heard the anguished cries of the mother who reached out for her four-year-old son just as the flood dragged him through the window and into the river. I heard the anguished cries of the father who tried to save his two daughters from the Pueblo flood. I could see his desperate efforts in my mind as he tried to keep them in his sights, reaching for them, grabbing their tiny, cold, wet hands, feeling them slip from his tight grip that could never be as strong as the force of the water. This was, by far, the most painful, difficult piece of writing I have ever completed, and I pray each night for the victims and survivors of these disasters.

It is never easy to write about floods, particularly flash floods. They come without warning, often in the darkness of night or the darkness created by massive clouds filled with rain. They are unpredictable—if they could be predicted, we would not have victims. They are far too common. Floods can occur in any area that has rain, which includes every state in our nation. On the list of natural disasters causing death and destruction, floods come in second behind tornadoes in the United States.

Complacency is human nature. We feel particularly safe and secure in our homes surrounded by family, pets, possessions and memories. But complacency can be dangerous. I learned as a child that closing the curtains to obscure the view does not keep the water from creeping into your home. It can happen to anyone, and the only defense is to be prepared.

# INTRODUCTION

*We cannot stop natural disasters but we can arm ourselves with knowledge: so many lives wouldn't have to be lost if there was enough disaster preparedness.*
—*Petra Nemcova*

There is a reason for this book and a reason why it was written at this time in Colorado's history. The state is experiencing a population explosion. With any dramatic rise in population and expansion of cities comes an increase in the chances of deaths and monetary losses due to natural disasters. For example, Weld County is the largest county, by size, in the United States, but it is also farm country with a traditionally low population. According to meteorologist Mike Nelson's *Colorado Weather Almanac*, Weld County has more tornado touchdowns than any county in the state. In years past, farmers suffered the most from these storms through the loss of crops. However, as more people move to Weld County, building houses, business and schools, the possibility of catastrophic losses from natural disasters increases greatly.

Colorado's landscape, including the towering Rocky Mountains and clear blue streams, leaves much of the state prone to the most dangerous type of flood: flash flood. In a flash flood, the water moves with shocking speed, destroying everything in its path and without warning. Colorado's flood history shows that this lack of warning creates the greatest danger to residents, particularly in the Foothills. Unfortunately, Colorado is not unique in this respect.

# Introduction

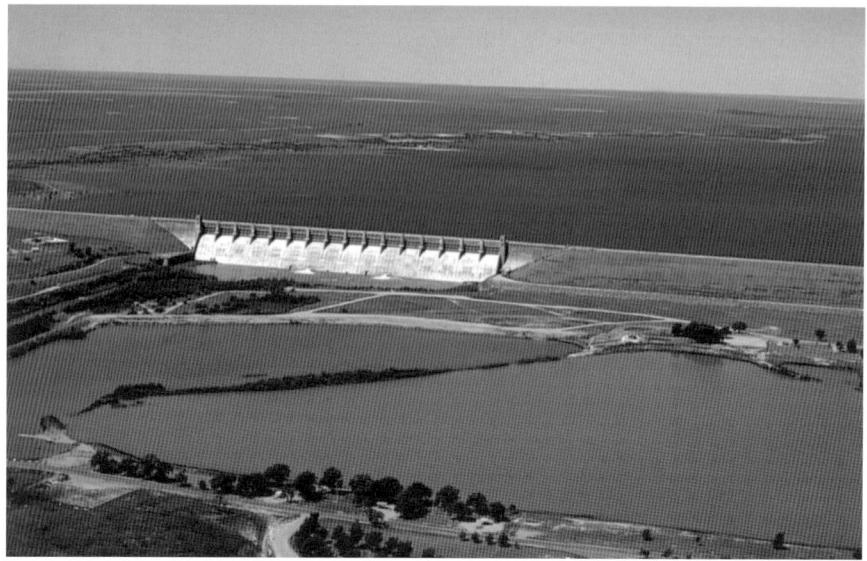

John Martin Dam and Reservoir on the Arkansas River in Bent County, Colorado. The dam was constructed by the U.S. Army Corps of Engineers for flood control on the Arkansas River. *U.S. Army Corps of Engineers.*

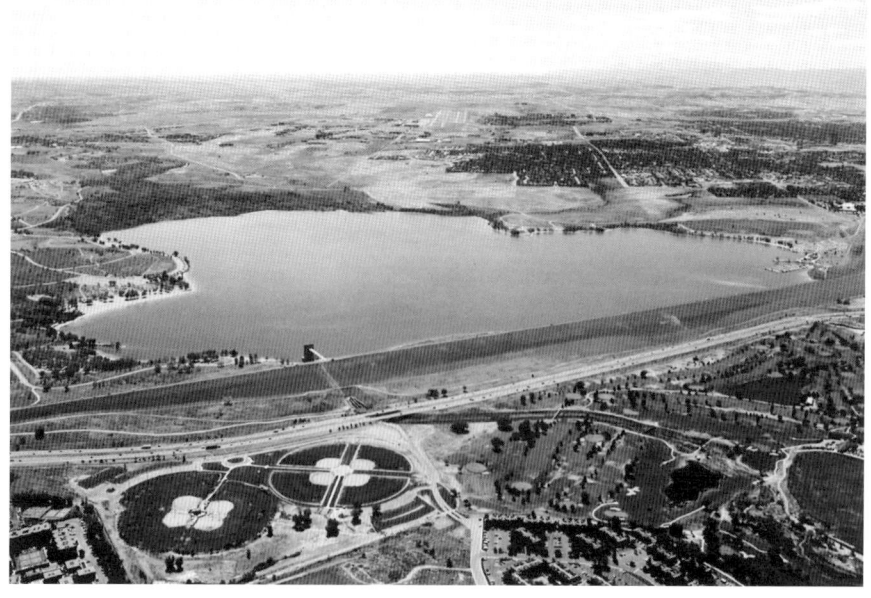

Cherry Creek Dam and Reservoir (Cherry Creek Lake) in Arapahoe County, Colorado. The dam was constructed by the U.S. Army Corps of Engineers and completed in 1950. The view is looking south across the dam and reservoir. *Photo by Harry Weddington, U.S. Army Corps of Engineers.*

Introduction

While many sources claim that tornadoes cause more deaths than any other natural disaster, a surprising claim from the National Severe Storms Laboratory states that more people die each year in the United States from floods than from tornadoes, hurricanes or lightning. A 2014 article in *Insurance Business America* lists Colorado as number nine in the list of top ten disaster-prone states. According to the Colorado Department of Homeland Security website, "flood prone areas have been identified in 268 cities and towns and in all of the 64 counties in Colorado. Using information supplied from local units of government, there are estimated to be approximately 250,000 people now living in Colorado's floodplains."

## A FEW FACTS ABOUT FLOODS—AND SOME ADVICE

There are a few things to keep in mind about floods. This information may save the lives of everyone in your family.

- Six inches of water can knock a grown man off his feet.
- Do not walk through water that is moving across roads and bridges. Turn and walk away. If you have a phone, call the police and report the flooding.
- Two feet of water is enough to carry a car, truck or even a bus into floodwaters.
- Avoid driving in storms at night, when it is more difficult to see flood dangers.
- Do not camp or park near creeks, streams, rivers or any body of water that might flood, and check the weather before making camping plans. This is a lesson made explicit from the stories in this book.

## BE PREPARED

In spite of the dangers and the unpredictability, there are steps residents can take to prepare for flooding. The American Red Cross, FEMA and the Department of Homeland Security all have detailed information on preparing for flood disasters.

# Introduction

One of the most important statements of advice concerns learning the difference between watches and warnings, and this generally applies to all natural disasters. A watch means a natural disaster is possible, that conditions are ripe for a disaster and residents should begin to prepare. A warning means that the disaster is already occurring and it is time to seek shelter or, in the case of floods, find higher ground.

If a watch has been issued, this is a good time to check the emergency kit and evacuation plan and to make certain the household is prepared for a possible warning. If there are large animals or livestock on the property, this is also the time to take them to a safe place—never wait for a warning to try to move horses or other animals. There will not be enough time.

Make a list of everything you might need if evacuated to a shelter, then build an evacuation kit. This could include everything from flashlights and batteries to toothbrushes, candles, matches or lighters and bottled water. These kits should be personalized—if there is someone in the family who requires medications, then an extra supply should be in the kit. Keep the kit in a place where it can be accessed within seconds, such as on the top shelf of the coat closet. Do not forget supplies for pets. In fact, it is a good idea to keep pet carriers next to or near the emergency kit so that everything can be accessed at the same time.

Write down an evacuation plan and discuss it with every member of the family. Keep the plan in a visible place, such as taped to the refrigerator. Remember to include the pets in the evacuation plan. Share the plan with family members who live outside the home or in different states and include communications in the plan—if it calls for going to the home of a neighbor, friend or another family member make certain that everyone knows.

Many homeowners don't realize that flooding is not covered by standard homeowner's insurance. Check with your insurance agent.

If there are important documents or items you cannot live without, keep them together and close to the front door so you can grab them and leave without having to search. Family photographs that cannot be replaced should be downloaded onto computers and stored online, but the originals can be stored and kept in one place, possibly near the emergency evacuation kit.

There is often a shortage of weather radios for sale after a natural disaster. These should be purchased now, not after they are needed and stored with the evacuation kit along with extra batteries. It's a good idea to keep an extra weather radio in the family vehicle along with a first-aid kit in case you are forced to leave the vehicle during a flood.

## Introduction

Even if the family vehicle is stocked, in the event of a flood, always leave the vehicle and climb to higher ground. Most of the victims in the Big Thompson Flood died in their vehicles; it is believed they could have survived if they had left their vehicles and climbed the mountainsides instead of trying to escape in their cars.

After a flood, avoid walking in floodwaters both inside and outside the home—there is no way of knowing what is in the water or beneath the surface.

If there is time, fill sinks and bathtubs with water in case you are trapped inside your house and drinking water is unavailable. Keep an axe in your home in case you need to chop a hole in the roof to climb out of your home. Turn off the utilities and unplug appliances. Stay informed and be prepared—it could mean the difference between life and death for the entire family.

# 1

# DENVER, GONE IN A FLASH

## THE GREAT FLOOD OF 1864

*Who knows, positively, if the Great Flood of 1864 would not have left Denver unharmed, if Denver had not obstructed its passage?*
—William B. Vickers

Gold, like water, changes the landscape so quickly that it becomes unrecognizable in the beat of a pounding heart—in a flash. Gold drew people to Denver, like mythical Sirens calling in their dreams. It was gold that inspired them to pitch their tents and build their hovels and homes on the banks of Cherry Creek*f*. In the spring of 1864, the water that hid the gold that had drawn people from all parts of the earth in just a few short years slammed into the town with the force of a prospector's pickaxe, as if seeking to reclaim its riches.

### DENVER'S GROWING PAINS

The city of Denver was built on the backs of miners. It was a gold rush town. To be exact, it was a collection of gold rush towns. The first yields of gold were small, but that was enough to attract the predictable flood of people. Numerous camps were established and merchant buildings constructed on the banks of Cherry Creek. The first people to enter gold camps were transient miners seeking quick money and merchants who provided tools,

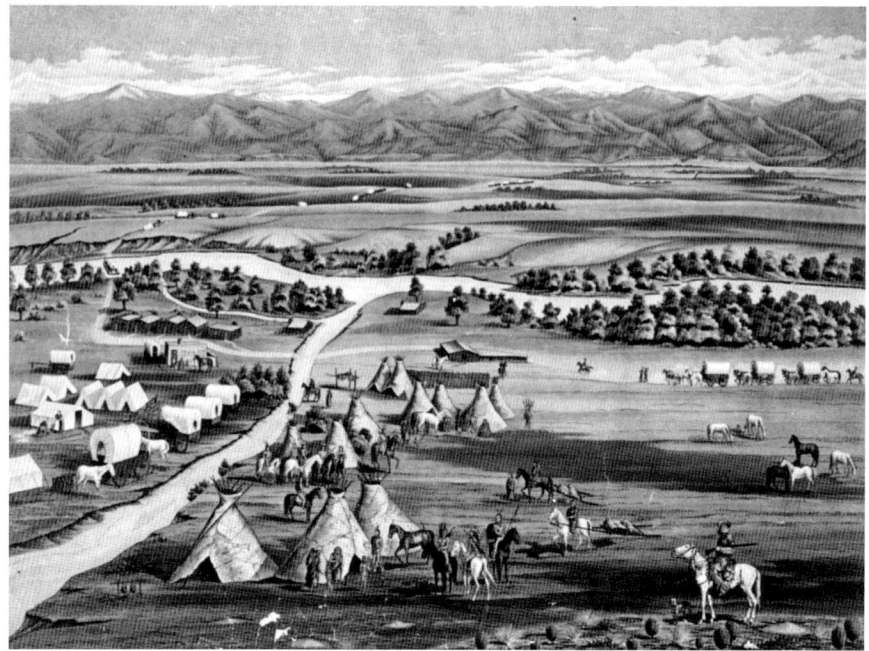

Denver, Colorado, in 1859, just before the gold rush. *Library of Congress.*

food, tents and other temporary shelter for the gold seekers, as well as entertainment in the form of alcohol, prostitutes, gambling and news. And word of the availability of supplies and entertainment attracted mountain men, trappers and explorers. In the 1800s, even the whisper of the word *gold* was enough to attract dreamers from around the world.

Tracking the population was a challenge. Even after the gold was believed to be tapped out, miners continued to arrive, alone or with their families in tow, acting on their dreams, their hearts filled with hope. As they entered the towns, they passed the miners and merchants who were giving up and going home—the people who were grossly unprepared or could not cope with the hardships found in gold camps. They were contemptuously referred to as "Go Backs" by William N. Byers, publisher of the *Rocky Mountain News*, which was founded in 1859.

## WILLIAM N. BYERS

Byers, like most Old West publishers, followed the rumors of gold. A former deputy surveyor for the Nebraska Territory, he bought a secondhand printing press from the defunct *Bellevue Gazette*. Byers understood from experience that gold rush towns were dependent, for many reasons, on newspapers. When he arrived at his destination with his printing press carefully preserved in an oxcart, Denver was still a collection of mining camps on the banks of Cherry Creek in Kansas Territory.

William N. Byers and his *Rocky Mountain News* came to symbolize the resilience of the city of Denver. In *The Townsmen*, Keith Wheeler explains that Byers originally rented the attic room above Uncle Dick Wooten's Western Saloon. The attic room had a leaking roof with no shingles, and snow fell for days, melting on the paper and the printing press, but Byers and his men only worked harder. Byers was on one side of Cherry Creek. His only competition, Jack Merrick, who arrived in Denver at the same time with the same intention—creating Denver's first newspaper—worked in his cabin on the opposite bank to print the first issue of the *Cherry Creek Pioneer*.

People from the town began to crowd into the doorways of Merrick's cabin and Byers's attic, placing bets and shouting encouragement. Byers was forced to send a man onto the roof to place a tarp over the holes as the water flowed like a stream onto the equipment.

In the early hours of April 23, 1859, William Byers ran from his attic with damp, smudged copies of his first issue of the *Rocky Mountain News*. He beat the competition by less than twenty minutes. Greatly discouraged by the loss, Merrick sold his supplies to Byers for twenty-five dollars' worth of bacon and flour then left the business to become a prospector.

Following the race to publish, Byers became a vocal and powerful leader of the people. His experience with fledgling cities also made him aware of the value of a location. Byers was determined to see the mining camps join together to provide safety from Indian attacks. He understood the importance of taking a neutral stance in the situation, so he built his office in the center of the mining camps and constructed the *Rocky Mountain News* building on pilings in the bed of Cherry Creek. Unfortunately, the one danger Byers failed to see was the water rushing beneath his feet.

William Byers was anything but neutral and unbiased. His vitriolic commentaries reflected his enthusiasm for creating a city, but he often neglected to see the dirty side of mining. Most inhabitants in mining camps were horribly unprepared for the life they faced, and their early housing is a clue as to why these people and their town were so easily carried away by floodwaters. They had no sawmills or lumber for the framing of houses. Only a few buildings had wood floors, and these were generally businesses. Buildings could be purchased through mail-order catalogues and delivered by train, then wagon, to their final destination, but this was expensive, and travel to gold rush areas left miners with empty pockets.

Many of the miners started their lives in tents purchased upon arrival and slept in the dirt. Others shared rooms packed with beds on dirt floors. Early "homes" consisted of the ever-present dirt floors; roof timbers formed the sides. The roofs of these early buildings were covered in dirt and grass—a layer of earth six inches deep that did nothing to stop rain or snow.

Denver had a rough start. It was a violent place with a transient population. An imprudent financial decision by Governor William Gilpin sent the city into a financial tailspin from 1862 to 1863. In the spring of 1863, an unusually dry winter turned the makeshift houses into firetraps, and most of the city burned to the ground. True to his nature, *Rocky Mountain News* publisher William Byers rallied the people to rebuild. Denver was on the brink of a remarkable comeback—then the floodwaters came down the mountains.

## "HAILSTONES AS LARGE AS HEN'S EGGS..."

In May 1864, when the rain first started to fall, it seemed like a blessing to the townspeople, who still had the horrors of the conflagration of 1863 on their minds. But the rain continued to fall. These early rains were not a blessing— they were a warning. But only the farmers seemed concerned. According to Junius E. Wharton's *History of the City of Denver*, there was hail the size of chicken eggs and days of monsoon-like rains that destroyed freshly planted crops. The skies were dark for days, and the rain fell for nearly a week, saturating the ground and creating tiny, flowing streams in fields.

On May 19–20, 1864, the water took back the land, along with the city and its people. According to Major Simeon Whitely's *Daily Commonwealth and Republican*, the first alarm came in the form of a ferocious roar as if a giant beast were tearing through town. The people of the city were confused by the sounds. They could not tell if these were sounds from the terrible storm, a tornado or a massive flood. The answer came quickly in the form of a wall of water.

Most sources state that the flood hit Denver sometime between 11:30 p.m. and midnight. It hit with an explosive crash as the force of the water and debris from higher up the river knocked down trees, which then served as battering rams against buildings, houses and anything else standing in the way. A group of men trapped inside the *Commonwealth* building tried to document the path of the flood by the cloud-blurred moonlight. They watched, horrified, as the building was quickly surrounded by water "washing with wildest fury on every side, carrying upon its uneven surface masses of flood wood, houses, fences, gigantic cottonwood trees, and driving before its current…huge boulders, which created a dull rumbling sound, that rendered other sounds still more frightful."

Some survivors said the wall of water was as high as thirty feet. Denver historian William B. Vickers believed the wall was much lower, though he does note that there was a tremendous amount of debris in the water that would have caused it to rise, as well as numerous buildings blocking the passage of the flood that we now know would have raised the height of the water in a similar fashion to water passing between canyon walls.

*Commonwealth* journalist and schoolteacher O.J. Goldrick described the disaster in a news article days later. The first building destroyed by the flood was the Methodist Episcopal Church, which was taken along with the

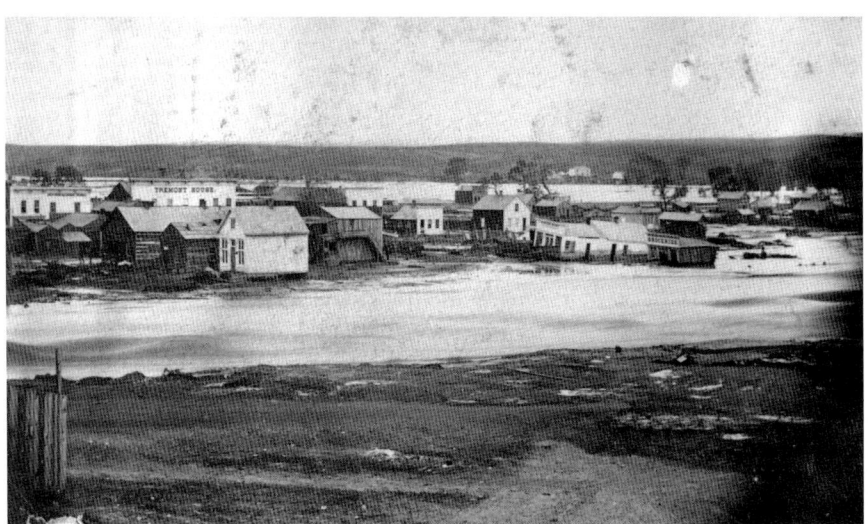

Denver during the 1864 Cherry Creek Flood. *Public domain.*

Larimer Street bridge, followed by the blacksmith's shop. The Methodist church and its adjoining buildings were seen smashing into the McGaa Street Bridge, which was then destroyed, followed by Mr. Charles and Mr. Hunt's law offices.

Goldrick states that Mr. C. Bruce Haines was sleeping naked in the law office when he was swept into the floodwaters and killed. However, Haines may have lost his clothing in the deluge. The force of the water in a flash flood, tsunami or any fast-moving body of water and the battering by debris can strip a person of every thread of clothing. It's possible that this is what happened to Haines, as he was in one of the first buildings struck by the wall of water, trees and boulders before the flood spread out across the land.

J.L. Dailey, who was William Byers's partner at that time, was still in the *Rocky Mountain News* building along with four employees. They escaped out of a side window using ropes for part of their rescue, then swam to reach the shoreline in time to see the building collapse. The *News* building crashed to the ground at 12:45 a.m.

## THE CHANGING LANDSCAPE

The landscape around the river was quickly changing, and the people of Denver scrambled onto newly formed sandbanks, clinging to one another in fear. Goldrick's account mentions the plight of both victim and survivor. From his position on one of these moving sandbars he saw "human beings buffeting with the billow crests and beckoning us to save them."

Around 2:00 a.m., as the men from the *Rocky Mountain News* office picked their way to the sandbanks, they suddenly realized that the water was rising again. Goldrick also noticed the rise in the water and its consequences. "Higher, broader, deeper and swifter boiled the waves of water, as the mass of flood, freighted with treasure, trees and livestock leaped toward the Blake street bridge, prancing with the violence of a fiery steed stark mad."

In his news article describing the events, Goldrick quoted Milton's description of Death in *Paradise Lost* as a metaphor for the horrific scene before him: "fierce as ten furies, terrible as hell."

The great waves were eating away at the sandbars, and the people on the banks began to speak their fears out loud, wondering if these were their last moments. Goldrick stood among the survivors watching the sand banks shrivel and described the moment as "inconceivably awful to behold."

## A DECEPTIVE BREAK IN THE STORM

Without explanation, the water levels began to drop. The people trapped in homes and buildings tried to leave for higher ground. Women were seen moving slowly through the icy waters, screaming for help with their children in their arms. Soldiers from the First Colorado Cavalry tried to assist in the rescue by riding into the flood on their horses.

Parents moved their children into the *Commonwealth* building for shelter, but the structure was thought to be unsafe by the men who had earlier evacuated. These families were rescued by the cavalry, as well. One of the cavalrymen nearly lost his life by swimming in the water trying to save a small boy. Other cavalrymen used their horses to move newspaper files and equipment from the *Commonwealth* building to higher ground.

Meanwhile, the small group of men from the *Commonwealth* managed to travel from one sandbank to another until they found shelter in the Tremont House, a popular hotel. In her book *Denver: An Archeological History*, Sarah M. Nelson used advertisements from that period to determine that the hotel was eventually surrounded by floodwaters and required renovation before reopening but had no permanent structural damage. This is confirmed by the stories of the men from the *Commonwealth* who claimed that as soon as they arrived at the Tremont, the floodwaters began to rise again, taking more houses, animals and people, but leaving the Tremont intact.

Many of the men of the city had left their families to move from one sandbar to another, trying to see if their homes were destroyed, if anyone

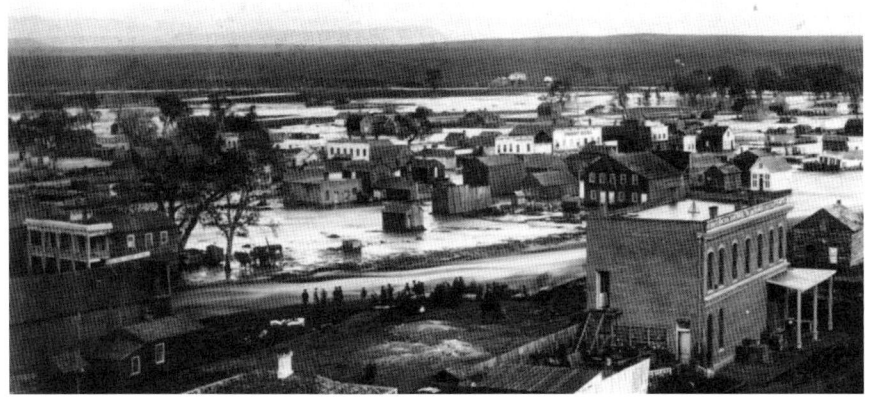

Crowds gather on the sandbars created by the Great Flood in Denver, May 19, 1864. Photo shows the view west of Cherry Creek. *Public domain.*

else could be saved or to retrieve possessions. When the waters began to rise once more in the Platte River, their families were warned to evacuate to higher ground. The warning sparked a panic among the women and children, and the men raced across the sandbars, trying to outrun the flood to once again help their families find safe ground.

## THE MORNING AFTER

As the sun rose, the people of Denver had their first look at the flood damage. Quartermaster Mullen's building was undamaged, and he invited the survivors to climb onto his roof and view the city. Goldrick described a scene of chaos and destruction. The floodwaters continued to flow down Cherry Creek and Platte River and through the city streets. He described a new river flowing down Cherry and Ferry Streets, the water filled with houses, livestock and household possessions "sailing at the rate of twenty miles or more an hour towards the Missouri River."

Families and friends tried to communicate with one another in spite of the water dividing them—there was still five feet of water flowing through the city. Survivors wrote letters on whatever paper they could find and tied the letters to rocks. The strongest among them tossed the rocks across the floodwaters.

## FLOODWATERS TRAP WILLIAM BYERS AND FAMILY

The survivors were able to find safety in the daylight and move to higher ground. Then word came that *Rocky Mountain News* publisher William Byers and his family were trapped in their home, surrounded by water. Colonel John Chivington (the same Colonel Chivington who would lead the horrific Sand Creek Massacre later that year) was a good friend of William Byers.

Chivington responded to the news of Byers's plight within minutes, urging his horse through the floodwaters to the Byers home. Byers told Chivington that his home could only stand another two-foot rise. Chivington raced back to the banks and enlisted the survivors in constructing a boat to rescue the family. The boat was sent to the Byers home, and the founder of the *Rocky Mountain News* and his family were taken to high ground.

# Colorado's Deadliest Floods

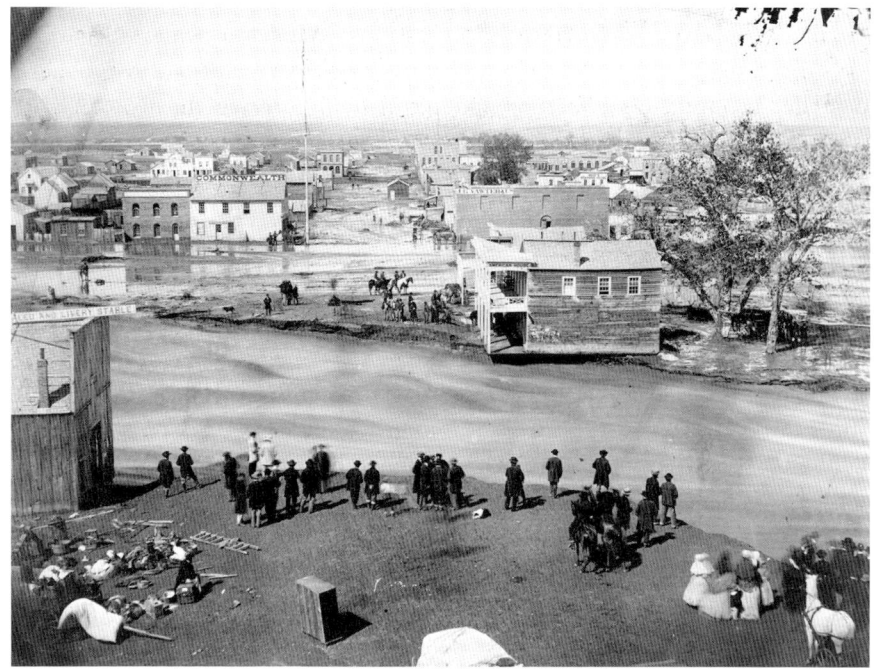

Survivors of the Great Flood in Denver, May 19, 1864, gather on a sandbar next to Larimer Street waiting for rescue. *Library of Congress.*

## A MORBID SIGHT

Reports came in slowly of the damage and the dead. Bodies were seen draped over tree branches and floating on wood in the river. Goldrick tells of a Mr. and Mrs. Smith who were carried off in the flood along with their five children. He praises Mrs. Smith for her bravery in saving her family but does not report how this was accomplished or if the entire family was saved.

As mentioned before, C. Bruce Haines, secretary of the Territorial Council, was drowned in the flood. His body was found far downstream near the home of another resident. The four-year-old son of the Fisher family also died in the flood, according to Goldrick. Mr. Rosenbaum, one of the men in the *Commonwealth* building, was at the front of the building on the lower floors when the flood struck. He was later found dead.

John Wall, a member of a special police force, was in the city hall when the flood struck. He remained in the building as it floated downriver and escaped to safety by leaping from the building and climbing into a tree on a sandbank. Denver resident J.M. Veasey chose to remain in his home when the floodwaters came. His house was torn from its foundation and twisted and turned about in the water, but it remained upright. The house finally drifted onto a sandbank, and Veasey escaped to higher ground.

## WILLIAM N. BYERS ALWAYS LANDS ON HIS FEET

After the flood of 1864, recovery was slow, but not for William Byers. His *Rocky Mountain News* was the first business to recover. Byers lost his printing press, and according to Keith Wheeler's *The Chroniclers*, parts of the original *News* printing press were found in Cherry Creek thirty-five years after the flood.

Byers also lost all of his supplies and his subscriber list in the flood, but he still had his home and savings. He used what he had left to purchase the building, printing press and supplies of the first newspaper to report his demise, the *Commonwealth*.

In the debut issue from his new location Byers reported that the "spasmodic stream called Cherry Creek is now entirely dry, and its broad channel's sands once more glistening in the sunshine." The *Rocky Mountain News* is believed to be Colorado's longest continuously running business. After receiving numerous Pulitzer Prizes for feature writing and photography, the paper printed its final issue on Friday, February 27, 2009.

## AN OMINOUS WARNING UNHEEDED

The *Commonwealth* news article ends with an anecdote about mountain man Jim Bridger. Bridger was famous as a mountain man who often resided with various Indian tribes, had numerous wives and lived an exciting, though controversial, life. He traveled on expeditions with Kit Carson, George Armstrong Custer, John Frémont and other famous men. Nevertheless, he did have a reputation as a "storyteller." (It's possible the reporter confused Bridger with James Beckwourth, another famous Colorado mountain man, explorer and storyteller).

In 1861, three years before the terrible flood, Bridger traveled with Lieutenant Edward Louis Berthoud to explore the Kansas Territory, possibly working as a guide. At that time, Bridger mentioned that he owned property in the gold towns near Cherry Creek but wanted to sell it because he thought it would soon become worthless. Other men in the exploration party disagreed, but Bridger insisted that the land along Cherry Creek was not as valuable as the men believed.

Bridger calmly explained that he traveled from Fort Laramie years earlier and discovered both the Cherry Creek and the Platte River deep with floodwaters with their banks overflowing. He was forced to camp on the opposite side of the Platte and waited nine days before he could cross. Bridger's companions doubted his story at the time, but many remembered the warning years later when the floodwaters came to Denver. As the people of Denver worked to rebuild their city, they were careful to give Cherry Creek a bit of land between its shores and the buildings and houses.

## AN ASSESSMENT OF TOTAL LOSSES

A complete assessment of damages and loss is impossible, due to the transient nature of the residents of Denver at the time and the destruction of account books in the flood. However, the residents of the city did attempt to document the total damages from the cost of rebuilding and the bodies that were located. Of the known residents and travelers in Denver at the time, at least twenty lives were known to be lost when their bodies were later recovered.

O.J. Goldrick reports that hundreds of ranches—not acres, but ranches—along with crops, livestock and outbuildings were lost along both Cherry Creek and the Platte River. One report stated that at least 4,500 sheep were found dead. There was not a count for cattle, chickens, pigs and other animals.

The Methodist Episcopal Church was the first building seen in the floodwaters. City hall was destroyed. Most of the town's homes, shops and businesses were lost. It is estimated that the residents of the city suffered at least $1 million in damages and loss of property, although numbers vary by source.

The May 19–20, 1864 flood was the first documented major flood in the city of Denver. However, in July 1878, Denver experienced another catastrophic flood. By that time the city had thirty thousand residents and numerous banks, schools and churches. The *Colorado Springs Gazette* reported

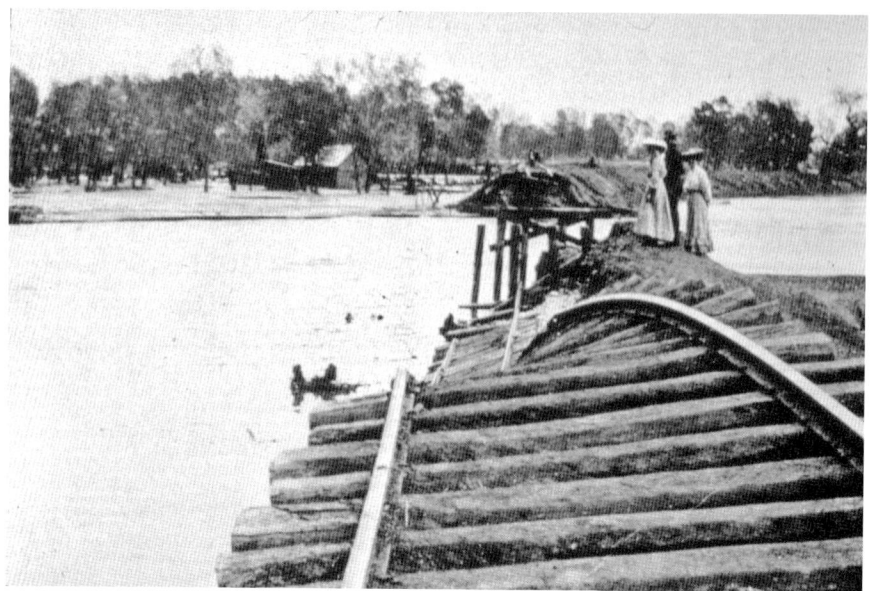

Cherry Creek flooding in the 1800s. *Courtesy of Colorado Department of Natural Resources.*

several damaged buildings, seven destroyed bridges and three deaths. Damage was estimated at $100,000 in 1878 ($1,468,280 adjusted).

The residents of Denver decided to take action to prevent future floods or to mitigate damage. They tried to change the river itself, guiding Cherry Creek in a western direction. The project was stopped by an injunction from Arapahoe County, which lies to the west, but a similar attempt to change the flow of the Big Thompson River in the Big Thompson Canyon proved the dangers in changing a river's natural path.

## WHERE DID ALL THAT WATER COME FROM? A QUICK LOOK AT THE WEATHER

Cherry Creek is actually a tributary of the South Platte River. According to the National Weather Service, the flood of 1864 was caused by heavy and continuous rain and hail over the Palmer Ridge in the Cherry Creek and Plum Creek basins. After days of heavy rains, the ground became saturated and the rainwater flowed into the creek and the river. It's possible that the reported rise and flood of the waters came from even more rain falling over Palmer Ridge.

# 2
# THE GROWL OF THE BIG BEAR

## THE BEAR CREEK BASIN FLOODS OF 1896
## AND A HISTORY OF FLOODS IN THE BEAR CREEK BASIN

*Think of your child, then, not as dead, but as living; not as a flower that has withered, but as one that is transplanted, and touched by a Divine hand, is blooming in richer colors and sweeter shades than those of earth.*
—Richard Hooker, British theologian

Weaving through the mountains southwest of Denver and near the city of Morrison is a tributary of the South Platte River called Bear Creek that flows into Bear Creek Lake. Oddly, in an area once famous as a camping and fishing site, Bear Creek is also notorious for deadly flash floods. Since July 1896, Bear Creek has been the source of twenty-four catastrophic floods, but the event of 1896 is remembered as the flood that made the mothers cry. It will always be remembered for the shocking number of children swept away to their deaths in the dark, fierce, cold waters of Bear Creek.

Two days after the disaster, the *Rocky Mountain News* printed a description of the flood that was picked up by newspapers statewide: "Morrison was considered the most delightful, quiet and peaceful summer resort in Colorado. Today it is a mass of wreckage and ruin, the people panic-stricken and a number of those who were inhabitants are either lying at the morgue, awaiting burial or are buried under an enormous mass of debris…never to be found until Gabriel sounds the last trumpet."

## A PARENT'S NIGHTMARE

July 24, 1896: the height of summer. The Bear Creek watershed, a favorite camping site for tourists as well as Colorado residents seeking peaceful nights with nature, slowly filled with tourists. There were hundreds of people camping and living near Bear Creek that night. The vacation cottages and cabins at the creek were all rented.

The banks of Bear Creek near Morrison were lined with tents filled with sleeping campers. Sergeant Dennis Potter of the Jefferson County Sheriff's Department, quoted in a study by the Urban Drainage and Flood Control District, said he counted at least fifty tents set up in a public park near Morrison. There were cottages and houses on the riverbanks and numerous barns and other structures on the properties of nearby homes belonging to permanent residents.

The swift, fierce, deadly flash floods of Colorado are unpredictable, so there is rarely enough time to warn anyone in their paths. The number of tents and structures counted before a disaster becomes vitally important when the disaster is over. Due to the number of people camped along the banks of the creek and the sudden, fierce cloudburst that sent a massive wall of water on the peaceful scene, it is impossible to estimate how many people died that night. There was not list of names or registrations for campgrounds. We can therefore assume that we will never know how many people died in the flood of 1896. We know who was reported missing, but we don't know who still lies buried beneath the mud and sand.

The flood was fast, deep and wide, and few managed to escape. However, one thing became painfully clear during the rescue and recovery efforts: most of the victims were children.

## A GRUMBLE, A ROAR, A CRASH OF THUNDER

It was Friday evening, one that future generations would refer to as Morrison's Black Friday. It was still early, around 8:00 p.m., when campers first heard sounds variously described as a grumble, a roar or a deafening crash of thunder, depending on the witness's proximity to the river. It was a cloudburst. A Colorado cloudburst.

Local ranchers knew the sound and the potential severity of the storm but perhaps underestimated the danger. Robert Follansbee, writing for the United

States Geological Survey (USGS), described the effects of the storm on a young woman who was riding her horse, checking the family's livestock: "By the time she reached the barn she was practically unconscious on her horse, and had to be revived by means used for resuscitating victims of drowning, as the intensity of the rain made it almost impossible for her to breathe." This was not an ordinary storm for many small towns in the United States, but, according to Follansbee, it was typical of a Colorado cloudburst.

Gradually, the sounds changed from thunder and lightning to a grumble and a roar. According to an article in the *Rocky Mountain News*, a few of the longtime residents quickly recognized the sound as that of a flash flood. They sent a young man to run to a set of cabins built close along the riverbanks. He stopped when he saw the ten-foot wall of water moving toward him and ran for higher ground. There was nothing he could do but watch as the tragedy began to unfold.

Flash floods are often called "walls of water" because that's how they appear to survivors—a wall shoving its way forward. They are often seen in cloudburst situations, and this was the first thing the young man saw: a giant wall tumbling toward him. Then he saw the victims. The first victim he recognized was his neighbor Elizabeth Miller, the young mother of three children. She was standing on the porch of her cabin. In a dreadful moment of irony, it was reported that Elizabeth was singing. She either heard the roar of the flood or saw the wall of water because she abruptly turned to run inside the cabin to save her children.

Elizabeth, her children and the Millers' cabin were tossed into the Wulff cabin next door, and the Millers' cabin exploded into pieces. The Wulff cabin was larger and filled with people. It remained intact when it was hit by the Miller cabin and started floating down the river. The young man, their would-be rescuer, continued to watch in horror as sixteen women and children ran for the windows and doorways, screaming and begging for help. But there was nothing anyone could do for them.

A neighboring farmer also saw the wall of water and climbed into a tree. He watched as the Wulff cottage floated past him. It crashed into a group of trees before it also exploded into splinters.

Vacationing families sitting in their cabins and tents were listening to the rain fall, completely unaware of their fate when the wall of water crashed into their shelters. The floodwaters obliterated the campgrounds, cabins and homes built on the riverbanks and slammed into the communities of Morrison and Golden, taking everything and everyone in their path. Screams and cries were heard coming from the creek, but nothing could be done in the extreme darkness.

According to witnesses, for one brief moment after the wall of water passed, there was a sickening silence.

## SEARCHING IN VAIN

When the floodwaters moved down the creek, the devastation surrounding the survivors was terrifying to behold. Parents and volunteers walked along the riverbanks with torches and lanterns, stumbling over uprooted trees and the remnants of buildings, bridges and even railroad tracks, shouting the names of their children into the darkness. Few answered in return.

The rescue work was difficult and painful, as all communication methods were destroyed. Survivors were found clinging to tree branches. Women and children were rescued from rooftops of homes floating in the water. Unfortunately, many women and children were found buried in the debris.

It was a cruel flood, a monstrous beast that seemed to seek out the helpless, ripping tiny children from their parents' grasps. At one moment, the small hand of a child gripped its father's hand as tightly as it could; in the next second, the child was gone. This is the reality of flash floods. This is the power of water. The parents of the children who died in the flood were filled with unbearable pain, anguish, guilt and remorse. Perhaps they wished they had disappeared into the floods with their children so their own suffering would end.

Nearly every member of four local families was killed in the Morrison flood—the Proctors, the Casey family, the Millers and the Herres family. S. Proctor was the president and manager of Denver Tent and Awning Company. His wife, Edith Proctor, was killed in the flood along with four of their children. The Proctors' twenty-year-old houseworker, Annie Hansen, was also killed. One of the Proctor daughters survived when two unidentified young men saw her clinging to a tree branch and climbed into the tree to rescue her from the floodwaters.

T.F. Casey of Denver lost his wife and five children, James, Edith, Mamie, Anna and Clara. Thomas McGough from Ohio, the twenty-one-year-old cousin of Mrs. Casey, also died.

Mrs. Anthony Herres, recently widowed, died, along with her four children, Eugene, Mabel, Josephine and Carol. The family's houseworker also perished.

Mrs. Moses Miller and her three children, residents of Morrison, were staying in a nearby cottage. Her husband was working farther up the river as a miner. Mrs. Miller and all of her children drowned.

The child of J.C. Longnecker, a Morrison resident, was found buried in the sand after the flood.

An article in the *Canyon Courier* newspaper of Evergreen, Colorado, stated that "two young girls were seen running for cover in a barn just before the structure was ripped apart by the flood." The two young girls were not identified, and their fate is unknown.

## A RIDE TO THE RANCH: THE SECOND FLOOD

On the afternoon of the day of the flood, the daughters of Judge J.W. Homer of Denver and a friend, Josephine Holme, whose father was the manager of the Denver Water Company, rode to the Lakewood Railroad at the Golden train station to meet their friends Mr. and Mrs. H.M. Warren Jr. of Brooklyn. The group of friends started toward the Homer ranch, located in Mount Vernon Canyon.

It had been raining since early morning near Evergreen. The air was somewhat cool and foggy. Dark clouds were marching from the direction of Morrison. The intensity of the rain increased as the day wore on, with a hailstorm beginning around 7:00 p.m. The rain and hail continued to pummel Evergreen for half an hour, but few of the residents thought to run for higher ground. Around 8:00 p.m., survivors reported seeing a wall of water between twenty-five and forty feet high burst through Tucker Gulch and into Clear Creek, carrying trees, shrubs, buildings and wildlife.

Like most victims, they had no warning of the danger. The bodies of all four women were found two hundred feet from their carriage. According to the *Sacramento Daily Union*, the women were found buried in sand. Mr. Warren was caught by the flood and found crumpled in a tree, injured but still alive. The bodies of the young women were returned to Denver to be identified and recovered by their parents.

## GOLDEN AND CLEAR CREEK

While the people of Morrison searched for their loved ones, residents of Golden were still listening to the rain. Golden was hit by a wall of water thirty feet high, according to the *Rifle Reveille*. It first hit the butcher shop, which was empty, then lifted the home of Mr. and Mrs. A.A. Johnson from its foundation and carried it along until it crashed into a bridge. The building smashed like kindling, killing both husband and wife as they tumbled into Clear Creek. Mrs. Johnson's body was found two hundred feet from her home, caught in the trees. Mr. Johnson's body was found much later near Coors Brewery.

Mrs. J.F. Edwards, a mother of two young children, had left her home to check on the barn animals. She was in her barn peacefully milking her cow when the waters carried the structure away, along with Mrs. Edwards and the animals inside. Her body was later discovered in Tucker Gulch.

James Bishop, who was eighty years old, was caught up in the floodwaters and desperately tried to save himself as he was swept downstream. He was caught in a tree and remained there for hours before being rescued. His ordeal was reported to have "unsettled his reason."

## LOSS OF PROPERTY

After the flood, the local church became a house of refuge for those who did not have family and friends nearby to offer shelter. There is no list of the many homes and farms destroyed by the floodwaters, but the loss was estimated to be in the thousands of dollars in Morrison alone. After the waters receded, the cities still had to cope with the loss of light and potable water. At least twenty-five bodies were known to be retrieved from the debris, but considering the count of the tents and cabins made prior to the flood, some estimate the number of victims to be closer to one hundred.

According to the National Oceanic and Atmospheric Administration's Western Water Assessment, flash floods occurred in Tucker Gulch, Mount Vernon Creek and Turkey Creek, all tributaries of Bear Creek, as well as in Clear Creek. There were twenty-nine known victims of the floods and $6,843,012 in (adjusted) damages.

The primary means of both personal and business transportation at that time was the railroads, which suffered extensive damage, particularly the

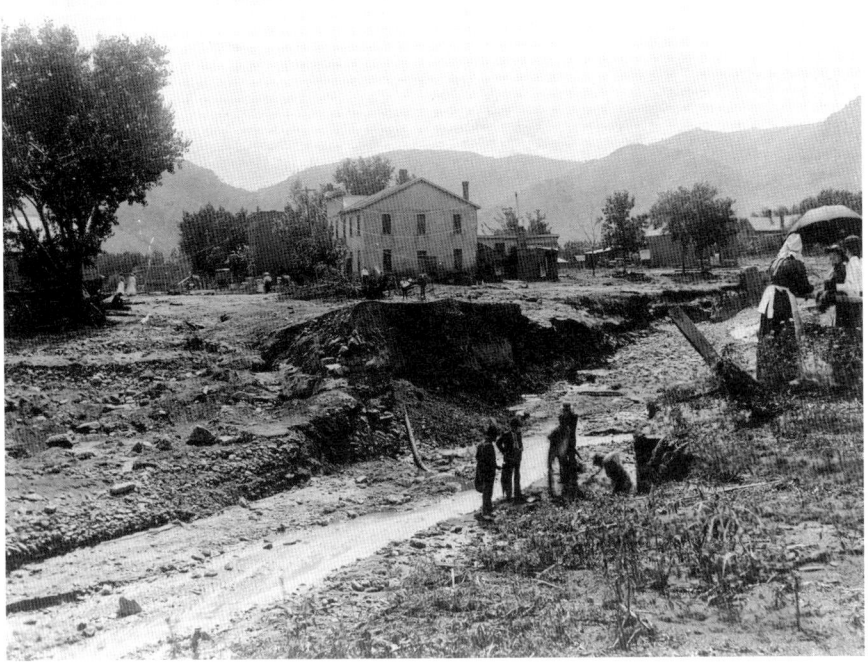

Townspeople survey damage from the July 24, 1896 Clear Creek Flood at Tenth and Ford Streets in Tucker Gluch, Golden, Jefferson County, Colorado. Two women with a child and umbrella stand at a wooden rail above the eroded riverbanks; several men below look for remains of the bridge. Debris and businesses show on Ford Street in the distance. *Golden History Museum City of Golden collection, courtesy of the Denver Public Library.*

tracks for the Denver & Rio Grande Railway. The Union Pacific, Denver & Gulf Railway near Golden was down for days. The tracks around Georgetown and Central City seemed to be the only ones left undamaged. However, the roads still needed to be cleared. Many of the boulders moved by the massive wall of water required the use of dynamite to be broken into smaller, moveable sizes and to make room for the stagecoaches.

## A LONG, SAD HISTORY OF FLOODING

The 2016 Urban Drainage and Flood Control District study on Bear Creek River Basin floods states that "since the 1860's there have been 24 known instances of floods in the Bear Creek basin that collectively have caused

45 deaths and considerable property damage. These floods occurred in 1866, two in 1878, 1885, 1886, 1893, 1894, 1896, 1903, 1907, 1908, two in 1921, 1923, 1925, 1933, 1934, 1938, 1946, two in 1957, 1965, 1969 and 1973."

Bear Creek connects with the South Platte River; both have a long history of creating flooding problems for Colorado residents. Most of these floods are due to the terrain, as well as to summer storms that are held in place for hours as they pour sheets of water into the rivers before moving on. A few of the floods are due to snowmelt in the spring, but summer storms cause the most concern.

One of the first recorded floods occurred from May 21 to 23, 1876. A journalist with the *Denver Tribune* reported his observations of the aftermath of the flood after spending days following the damage path along Bear Creek and its tributaries. The writer said he found that new gullies formed by the flood were as much as twenty feet deep.

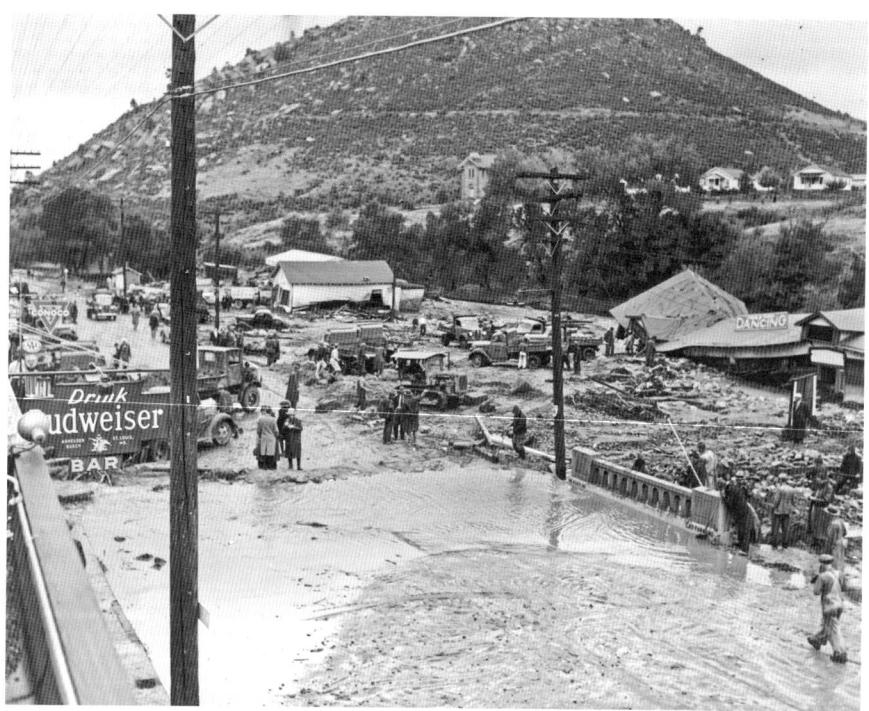

Flood damage in Morrison, Jefferson County, Colorado, in 1938 consists of standing water on the Mount Vernon Creek Bridge and the collapsed roof of a building with a sign: "Dancing." People, trucks, cars and bulldozers crowd the scene; the school is on the hill in the background. Signs read: "Drink Budweiser Anheuser Busch St. Louis Mo. Bar," "Conoco" and "AAA." *Courtesy of the Denver Public Library.*

## Colorado's Deadliest Floods

The flood of 1933 was created by an afternoon storm that left five people dead. At times, the wall of water reached as high as fifteen feet as it moved between buildings; the highway leading up Bear Creek Canyon between Mount Morrison and Idledale was destroyed. One year later, the same area was struck by another flood that took the lives of six people.

On August 30, 1938, a thunderstorm began over the eastern slope of the Front Range and stalled. It is believed to be the most intense storm the city of Morrison has experienced. The flooding began on September 2 and continued into the following day. At one point, 7.9 inches of rain fell near Morrison in six hours. When the floodwaters subsided and rebuilding began, the damage was estimated at $450,000.

Another flood in Bear Creek near Morrison occurred on August 24, 1946. The water rose so quickly that it trapped a woman in her vehicle, leaving her stranded and helpless. She eventually drowned.

On August 21, 1957, a series of thunderstorms once again struck the Bear Creek Basin near Morrison. Intense rain and hailstorms began around 1:00 p.m. and ended within an hour, but so much rain fell that by 3:00 p.m. the banks of the Bear Creek were overflowing. The primary area of damage was once again in Morrison. Debris left from the flood created a terrible mess in the city, and the flood broke a water main, which created engineering issues. Portions of State Highway 8 were closed due to flooding.

On July 25, 1965, Bear Creek experienced minor flooding, but residents of Morrison once again had to cope with damage to homes and property.

An extreme rainstorm that lasted from May 4 to May 8, 1969, caused additional flooding in Bear Creek and Morrison. Local weather stations reported an average of 5.77 inches of rain per day.

Will it end? Not anytime soon. The 2013 Colorado Floods caused severe damage to Bear Creek Lake. The lake is one of three in Colorado that has a U.S. Army Corps of Engineers dam designed to protect the city of Denver and surrounding areas from floods. The other two are Cherry Creek Dam and Chatfield Dam. After the 2013 flood, $372,000 was spent to repair the damage to Bear Creek Lake dam when the lake peaked at fifty feet above normal. According to an article in the *Denver Post*, in May 2015, Bear Creek Lake was once again at forty feet above normal.

# 3
# TERROR IN THE NIGHT

## THE EDEN TRAIN WRECK OF 1904

*I scarcely know how it happened, as I was dazed in the mud on the bank of the creek. I only know that there are dozens and dozens dead....It all happened so quickly—and, my God, it is so terrible.*
—*Fireman Frank Mayfield, survivor of the Eden Train Wreck*

The city of Pueblo was settled by Native Americans at the junction of the Arkansas River and Fountain Creek. The area has a long, exciting history as part of the American West, beginning with the French fur trappers in the 1700s. For many years, it was a wild, dangerous place, but its warm winters were attractive to settlers. By the late 1800s, Pueblo was thriving with industries and a population impossible to count due to the many workers attracted by the steel mill, smelting hub and huge rail yard. In southern Colorado, all tracks led to Pueblo.

Just outside Pueblo, numerous trestles—bridges built on stilts to support the train tracks—crossed over arroyos. These dry riverbeds, generally formed naturally, caught floodwaters and kept the trains and passengers safe as they traveled into Pueblo. One arroyo bridge, referred to as Hogan's Draw, is located near Eden Station, one mile north of Eden and approximately eight miles north of Pueblo, east of what are now the northbound lanes of I-25. The bridge is fifty feet wide and fifteen feet deep with steep banks. When the arroyo fills with water, flash floods often result. The arroyo empties into the Fountain River, which then empties into the Arkansas River.

## THE NO. 11 MISSOURI PACIFIC FLYER

It was mid-evening, 8:00 p.m. on August 7, 1904, when a late summer storm raged through southern Colorado. Around 7:00 p.m., the No. 7 train had passed over the No. 110 "B" bridge, crossing the arroyo and arriving safely in Pueblo. Then came the No. 11 Missouri Pacific Flyer, also referred to as "The World's Fair Flyer," according to Jay Nash's *Darkest Hours*.

The *Alamosa Journal* called the No. 11 Missouri Pacific Flyer the fastest passenger train owned by the Denver & Rio Grande traveling the Missouri Pacific connection. But on the night of August 7, the No. 11 was running six minutes behind, possibly due to the storm. Early news reports stated that the engineer was taking precautions because of a thunderstorm caution, but later investigations showed the train was actually traveling at its normal speed.

The No. 11 Missouri Pacific Flyer was pulling an express or passenger car, also known as the chair car; the smoker, in which passengers could smoke without disturbing other passengers; the diner car; and two sleeper cars, also known as Pullmans, after their inventor, George Pullman. The No. 11 had a surprising number of employees on board: the engineer, the fireman, a porter for each Pullman car, a Pullman conductor, the dining car conductor and six men working the dining car. The No. 11 had a steam engine, which explains the fireman working with the engineer. The fireman's job was to shovel coal into the furnace and tend the boiler.

The No. 11 generally had a large passenger load when traveling to Kansas City and St. Louis. On August 7, the load was around 125 persons, including many women and children. The majority of passengers on the train were from Denver and Pueblo. Every coach was filled, but neither the passenger load nor the speed of the train was a factor in what happened that night. It was the rain, the flood and the collapse of two bridges.

## SNOW IN SUMMER

On the night of August 7, 1904, at 8:00 p.m., dark, cold, fast-moving water filled the arroyo. It was a flash flood—sudden, fast, fierce and deadly, and with eerie timing. It missed the No. 7 train but filled the arroyo moments before the arrival of the No. 11.

Survivors reported that they both saw and heard signs of a severe storm and that some of the passengers became nervous. They saw lightning and heard thunder so loud it shook the train. A personal account by passenger O.S. Galbraith was published in the *Durango Wage Earner* on August 25, 1904: "When Fountain, a few miles out from Colorado Springs was reached, everything had the appearance of a recent rain, snow, or hail storm. It was just getting dark, and piles of either snow or hail were lying on the platform. It attracted the attention of several of the passengers in our coach, who, evidently, were not used to such a sight in August, and they were excitedly talking about the snow. I rather think it was hail, but did not examine it closely."

No, it was not snow in August. Colorado has a reputation for record-setting hailstorms. According to a CNN story, in July 2016, a storm with hail the size of tennis balls lasted for hours and left the city with the appearance of a snowstorm. A report from the *National Insurance Crime Bureau* stated that Colorado now ranks second among all states for the most hail-caused loss insurance claims. Hailstorms that appear to be snow storms are not new to the area through which the train passed, and hail from a severe and terrible storm is what the passengers saw when they stared out the window on that night in 1904. The engineer may have also been confused by white mounds covering the ground, not realizing as he moved the train forward that he was actually moving into a terrible storm.

## TERROR IN THE NIGHT

Most of the details about what took place in the engine that night came from fireman Frank Mayfield, who was reported to be in a state of shock and, according to the *Colorado Springs Gazette*, "almost insane" when he reached Pueblo.

It was initially reported that the engineer, Charles Hindman, received warning of a severe thunderstorm and was also warned that the storm had intensified. News reports state that the engineer took standard thunderstorm precautions and slowed the train to between ten and fifteen miles per hour, but an investigation into the disaster revealed that the No. 11 was behind schedule and was actually moving faster than storm conditions recommend. Initially, Mayfield recalled asking the engineer if they had enough coal in the boiler to make it to Pueblo. He was instructed to add more coal. Hindman was watching for washaways as they neared the bridge.

Mayfield reported two versions of what happened next. He initially told reporters that he was standing in the doorway with a torch watching for washaways with the engineer. At that point, Hindman must have seen the water tumbling beneath the train—it was at least fifteen feet high. He may have seen the water on the tracks, as well. The train was already moving at a fast rate—it was too late to slow it down. His last spoken words were to instruct the fireman to "Put out that torch," knowing the train was about to crash.

Just before the engine reached the opposite bank, a wall of water slammed into the trestle bridge and shoved the train cars to the right with such force it sliced through the coupling of the two Pullman cars and the dining car. Hindman may have attempted to apply the brakes. The engine fell back, dragging the baggage car, smoker and passenger car into the floodwater.

Engineer Charles Hindman was thrown into the water and debris. His body was later found in the muddy riverbank near Eden a mile from the crash site.

In a later account, Mayfield stated that he was not standing in the doorway with a torch. Instead, he was shoveling a second scoop of coal into the boiler. Mayfield told the *Colorado Springs Gazette*: "The engine gave a lurch upward. I lost my balance and was thrown from the train on the bank of the creek. I must have struck partly on my head, as I was dazed and did not know what happened for several minutes. When I came to I saw the Pullman cars standing near me, but could not see the engine or the rest of the train. I went up and down the stream looking for my partner, Charley, the engineer." Mayfield stated that he did not realize a shocking amount of water was flowing across the top of the bridge until he was tossed from the engine and could look at the bridge from outside.

The engineer was dead and floating in the water. The fireman was wandering on the far bank with a head injury. Most of the passengers were thrown into the floodwater with such intensity that they didn't have time to scream. They disappeared beneath the twisted metal and into the mud. The remaining passengers were still in their seats, wondering about the hard jolt, the sudden stop and the silence from the front of the train.

R. Brunazzi was the superintendent of the dining car service for the Denver & Rio Grande. Brunazzi felt the jolt of the water's impact, then the crash, then he felt the dining car turning. Brunazzi told the *Colorado Springs Gazette*, "I rushed to the platform and saw before me nothing but a black, raging torrent with three coaches whirling down the stream. It was horrible. I have never experienced anything like the awful sensation that came over me when

I saw the cars, packed with human beings, floating down that flood. The water was rushing against the banks with terrific velocity, and no human being, it seemed to me, could ever withstand that awful current."

Three men in the smoker noticed a hole in the roof of the car when it crashed down into the floodwaters. The men swam through the flooded train car to the hole and escaped into the water, then continued swimming until they reached the muddy bank.

## QUICK-THINKING HERO

W. Melville Sales, originally from St. Louis, was the porter for the second Pullman sleeper car. Sales may have seen what was happening or heard the slashing sound of crushing metal. Whether it was instinct or experience, Sales somehow knew the passengers were in danger. Acting without pause and with amazing speed, Sales pulled the emergency air brake, which instantly locked the wheels of the Pullman car. The Pullman car in front of him was left dangling over the raging waters. The actions of Sales saved the lives of the passengers who remained in his Pullman car and the remaining cars on the train.

O.S. Galbraith, who is quoted earlier regarding the hailstorm and its resemblance to snow, remained seated with the rest of the passengers. Galbraith was traveling with his daughter, Mrs. Everard Roscoe (Bessie Galbraith) of Goodlettsville, Tennessee, and his granddaughter, three-year-old Agnes. Galbraith had discussed the hailstorm moments earlier with his daughter.

Galbraith recalled that his daughter, feeling nervous about the trip, had commented on the unusual number of women and children on the train that night. When the train jerked to a sudden stop, father and daughter both became concerned, but the darkness and the storm kept the passengers in their seats. After approximately ten minutes, Bessie decided she wanted to find out what happened to the train. She walked to the front of the car and returned visibly distraught. She told her father that the engine was in the water. Galbraith thought she must have been mistaken and went forward to check for himself. He was horrified to see the first sleeper completely empty and dangling over the broken bridge.

## A DELAYED RESCUE

When fireman Frank Mayfield began to recover from his head injury, he ran for help. He met train operator Frank M. Jones and his wife. Jones was on watch that evening. He could barely see the lights of the train through the storm. He watched the lights as the train crossed the bridge, then the lights disappeared. He waited, hoping the lights would come back into focus, but they never did. Then he heard a sound. Was it a crash, or thunder? His wife heard it, too. They quickly gathered a few supplies and started walking beside the tracks in search of the train. Instead, they found Frank Mayfield. When help finally came, it was from Pueblo, hours later.

The surviving twenty-nine passengers, some with minor injuries, exited the train and huddled together in the darkness, whispering, hoping that the missing train cars and passengers made it to the opposite bank before the bridge collapsed. They occasionally shouted for help, but no one answered, so they spent most of their time together in silence. Eventually, the storm cleared and the stars came out, and the survivors built a fire for warmth. The floodwater was beginning to dissipate, the level of water slowly going down. According to Galbraith, the terrified survivors remained huddled

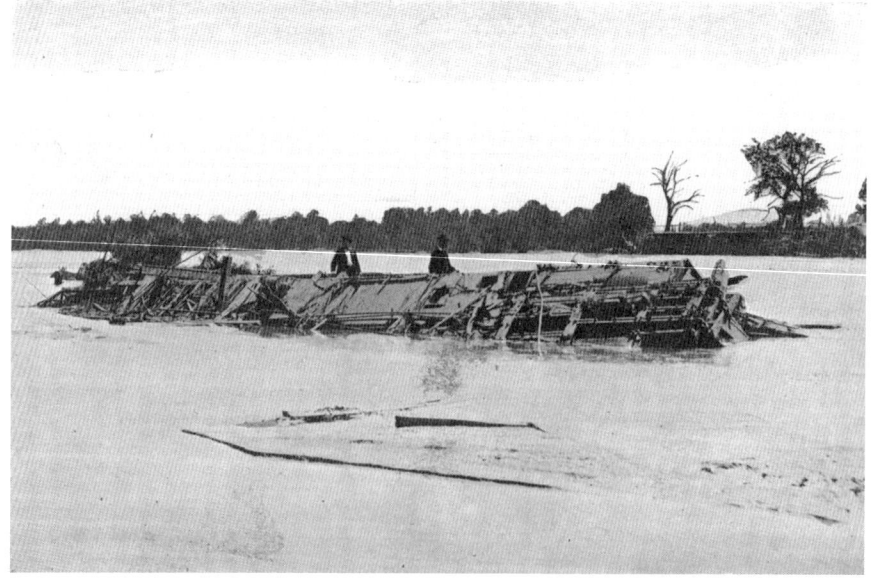

View of a Denver & Rio Grande Railroad wreck in Eden, Pueblo County, Colorado. Men are on an overturned passenger car surrounded by water. *Courtesy of the Denver Public Library.*

around the fire for four hours, then Galbraith noticed a man walking along the banks with a torch. Galbraith left the group and asked the man if he knew what happened to the train. The man replied with a nod, "Down there in the water."

A train arrived from Pueblo four hours later. The water was flowing from the arroyo much faster now, and the engine could be seen in the mud. The men built steps going down the riverbank and used scrap wood to build a footbridge so the survivors could cross to the other side and board the rescue train. Galbraith recalls his little granddaughter clinging bravely to her suitcase as she stared up at the train and said, "Oh, look at the pretty lights!"

It was not a terribly morbid sight for the survivors. The strength of the floodwaters was so intense that it had moved the victims and wreckage downstream almost immediately after the train hit the water.

It is known that it took a shocking amount of time for the rescue train to leave for the accident. The second train did not leave Pueblo until 11:00 p.m. that night, nearly three hours after the wreck. The rescue train had stretchers, coffins and police officers. There was also a "special train" that included as its passengers all available medical professionals and officials from the Rio Grande and Missouri Pacific, but there was little need for the doctors on board. The seventeen uninjured passengers arrived in Pueblo on the first train. The injured arrived on the second train. Most of the victims were killed instantly. The survivors arrived in Pueblo around 1:45 a.m. the following morning.

## THE MORNING AFTER

Most of the water left the arroyo within two hours of the flash flood, flowing into Fountain Creek. The creek was raging with muddy water and filled with debris and bodies from the wreck when the rescue trains arrived. This is where the five hundred men who traveled to the site the next morning concentrated their recovery efforts. They started their search with bloodhounds, but the dogs kept sinking into the quicksand, which made the recovery work even more difficult.

The *Akron Weekly Pioneer Press* reported, "Death to most of the passengers must have been sudden and in all probability painless. They were drowned. The bodies of those recovered show few bruises." The statement illustrates the sentiment of the times— a show of respect for the dead and their families.

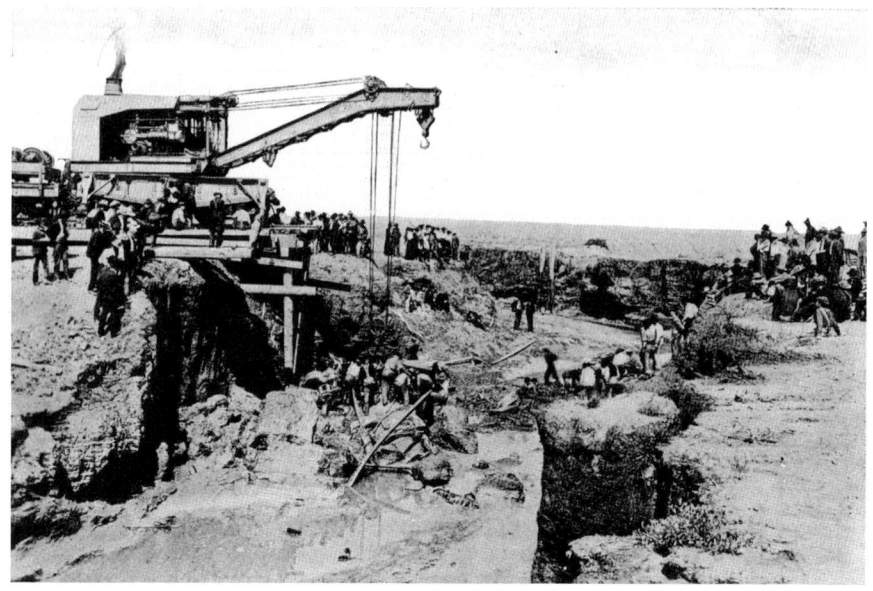

View of a Denver & Rio Grande Railroad wreck in Eden, Pueblo County, Colorado. Seen are workers, spectators, a crane and Dry Creek. *Courtesy of the Denver Public Library.*

In truth, there is nothing painless about being thrown into a raging torrent with twisted metal in a late-night thunderstorm and drowning in mud.

The following day, the engine was found lying on its right side. The chair, or passenger car, was in Fountain Creek half a mile from the wreck. At the time of the initial investigation on August 8, the baggage and smoker cars could not be located. Approximately thirty bodies of victims were recovered. By August 9, another seventy victims had been recovered.

The recovery effort was hampered by the fact that the debris and bodies were carried into Fountain Creek and buried in the mud and sand. The train cars were tremendously heavy, and victims were beneath the cars, which makes the comment by the *Akron Weekly* reporter even more dubious—rescue workers reported that the bodies of the victims were severely mangled, some beyond recognition. In truth, the passengers would have suffered tremendously beneath the weight of the train wreckage.

On August 9, 1904, the *Colorado Springs Gazette* gave what was perhaps a more accurate account of the scene after the wreck: "A hundred lives lost in a maelstrom of seething steam and roaring waters. Bodies torn and limbs shattered and human souls hurled into an eternity without warning."

## THE TERRIBLE AFTERMATH

When the recovery effort was completed, it was discovered that 111 passengers and crew members had died. The tragedy was reported nationwide to shocked and grieving Americans. It was one of the most horrific and deadly train accidents of the time.

The *Colorado Springs Gazette* reported the story of an elderly woman who walked the riverbanks for hours with two friends, sobbing, calling out, searching desperately for her loved ones. Most of the bodies were carried at least ten miles downstream. The bodies of fourteen victims were never found.

The bridge was quickly rebuilt, but the engine was buried so deeply in the muddy gulch that the bridge was built around the mangled wreckage. Express train No. 11 traveled over the repaired bridge within twenty-four hours of the disaster.

The day after the wreck, business came to a halt in Pueblo. There were four morgues operating in Pueblo at the time, and they were all full. But they were also packed with residents searching for missing family members. Carrie Bishop of Connecticut had been visiting her two cousins, John and Esther Bishop of Pueblo. All three were killed in the crash. In a strange twist of fate, Bishop's father had been killed in a train wreck the year before.

Kate Garland of Denver died with four of her children, ages two to eleven. The body of one of her sons was never found. Left behind were Mr. Garland and another son, Frank, who was not on the train.

One of the most widely publicized victim reports was that of an elegantly dressed young woman, twenty-five years old, whose body was discovered on the muddy banks of the Arkansas River twenty-five miles from the trestle bridge where she had fallen.

Nash's *Darkest Hours* states that the general public was shocked by what they believed to be an inappropriately casual manner used by a superintendent when he informed the Denver & Rio Grande headquarters that the train's safe was recovered and there was no theft of its content.

A morbid task that is sadly common in flash floods is that of gathering and identifying the personal belongings of the victims and returning the possessions to surviving family members. In the case of the Eden train crash, this included an abundance of luggage. According to the *Herald Democrat*, there was eight pieces of luggage awaiting identification after the flood. The final piece of luggage was claimed by Mrs. Peterson of Sams, Colorado, in San Miguel County. Peterson's husband was on the train that night. He had arrived in Denver on August 5 to meet with an agent of a correspondence school and, in an eerie coincidence, had also met with an insurance agent to open a life insurance policy.

According to a USGS report: "During the flood of 1921 the tributary streams had maximum discharges per square mile that were almost unprecedented in the Rocky Mountain States. The only recorded unit discharge that, equaled, them was that of Hogan's Gulch near Eden, Colo., a station on the Denver & Rio Grande Western Railroad between Colorado Springs and Pueblo." The strength of the storm, which was caused by a cloudburst, was ironically recorded at a station on the Denver & Rio Grande Western Railroad located between Colorado Springs and Pueblo.

## THE INVESTIGATION

The two Pullman cars and dining car were returned to Colorado Springs and examined, along with the rest of the evidence. According to the *Herald Democrat*, on August 20, 1904, a coroner's jury "censured" the Denver & Rio Grande Railroad after the jury determined that the railroad was guilty of negligence. The jury concluded that the bridge was of the wrong class and should have been sturdy enough to withstand the force of the debris from the first bridge that collapsed and was carried through the arroyo, which is logical considering that the purpose of an arroyo is to guide floodwater. The bridge—number 110 "B"—was considered of the highest class of bridges in the country, but it was the wrong type for use in an arroyo. It should have had "one strand with stone abutments" in order to withstand floodwaters and debris. A single span metal bridge could have handled the water.

The jury also determined that there should have been a regular system of track walkers. Such an employee would have seen the water moving over the bridge that night, flagged the train in advance and prevented the accident.

Finally, the jury decided that the crew was not to blame for any part of the disaster, as it was impossible for any crew member to see the water on the tracks ahead or to know that a nearby bridge had washed out. There were numerous lawsuits filed after the crash; the last was settled in 1929.

# 4
# CATASTROPHE AT CHERRY CREEK

## THE DENVER FLOOD OF 1912

*If they do it often, it isn't a mistake, it's just their behavior.*
—Dr. Steve Maraboli

Before the miners came, before the merchants and the prostitutes and the politicians arrived, they were warned. Mountain man Jim Bridger stated that he had witnessed the flooding of Cherry Creek firsthand. Some historians claim that Little Raven, chief of the Arapahoe Indians, warned the early explorers of flash flooding on Cherry Creek and told them specifically not to build on the land.

In 1864 and 1878, the city of Denver experienced catastrophic flooding—but the city continued to grow, and little was done to protect its residents from future floods. Some merchants and families moved to higher ground, but these moves were made to protect themselves, not the city as a whole. The floods would continue. It was inevitable. Some residents chose to move to safer building sites on higher ground, but this was not a citywide decision. Many residents and merchants remained in the danger zone.

Cherry Creek connects with the South Platte River two hundred yards above the Sixteenth Street viaduct in Denver, but its source is fifty miles south of Denver. It has always been a part of Denver, even before Denver was a city. Cherry Creek may be small, but it has a loud voice. In the 1800s, it called to people around the world to come in search of gold and build a city around that insignificant flow of water until, finally, the creek was just as much a part of Denver as its people, houses and businesses and Cherry Creek flowed through the very heart of Denver.

## A PEACEFUL MORNING BECOMES A DEADLY NIGHT

July 14, 1912, was a peaceful Sunday morning, and the residents started their day in their usual way, working their farms or going to church. As the day wore on, the clouds moved in over the Cherry Creek basin. Then the clouds turned black.

According to the Colorado Division of Homeland Security website, the rain began to fall around 3:00 p.m. The sky was black, and the storm was fierce. By 6:30 p.m., two inches had accumulated in Denver. The rain began in Castle Rock a bit later, around 5:00 p.m. The rain became a deluge for approximately half an hour, then it eased up. But there was still another inch of rain on the ground by 7:00 p.m.

The rain continued throughout the night as a soft drizzle that accumulated another inch in the river and creek. Some sources believe the rain was falling heavier in places that were not monitored by the weather bureau station because the amount of water flowing through town did not match the amount reported. Residents became concerned—the South Platte River had risen by three feet. Still, there was no sign that flooding was imminent.

## THE UNTHINKABLE

Then the unthinkable happened—a massive wall of water came barreling down Cherry Creek sometime between 8:30 p.m. and 9:30 p.m. on July 15, 1912. According to the *Pueblo Chieftain*, the initial wall was twenty-five feet high.

Many of the residents were unaware that the water was rising in the creek until it overflowed its banks around 10:00 p.m. and flowed like a river on the streets near the railroad and the Union Depot. The water was at least two feet above the city's bridges and two to three feet high in the depot.

The *Rocky Mountain News* reported a foot of water covering all of City Park. The retaining wall near city hall threatened to crash into the floodwaters, but it remained intact, and city hall was saved. Starting around 10:30 p.m., the water flowing in the South Platte River and Cherry Creek slowly returned to normal levels.

## CONFUSED AND BEWILDERED

There was so much sand left by the water that it destroyed all crops near the river and creek, decimating the city's food supply. The sand and silt filled gardens and parks. It covered streets and bridges. It flowed inside homes, office buildings and the shops of local merchants. It temporarily stalled the trains on their silt-covered tracks, and the tram was disabled for hours, bringing the city to a complete halt. The *Rocky Mountain News* reported that over one thousand people waited for streetcars to take them to safety, but the cars never arrived—a six-foot lake of water had formed at Twenty-Third Street and Colorado Boulevard, leaving the streetcars flooded and unusable.

## A MYSTERY

The Denver Gas & Electric Company struggled to repair damage and restore service to customers. The Bell Telephone Company was formed in 1877; by 1879, Denver businessman Frederick O. Vaille had managed to bring telephone communications to the city. This is the beginning of an intriguing mystery.

There is one mention in the *Kingston Daily Freeman* of a mysterious caller who alerted residents about the flood that night. However, the Mountain States Telephone Company was said to have had many lines out of commission. The identity of the telephone operator and the calls of warning are a mystery to this author.

Journalists understand the difficulties in establishing fact from fiction during and after natural disasters. They are seeking facts from people still suffering from extreme fear, disappointment and grief. There is also the fact that, within fifteen minutes of witnessing a traumatic event, a person begins to change that event, to add or remove details that do not logically fit with the witness's life experiences.

Did a mysterious person call residents and warn them of the flood? It is possible, and perhaps that person's name is written down somewhere. It may have been Vaille, who checked on his telephone lines then realized he could use this new form of communication to warn people and save lives. If it did happen, whoever it was that made those calls possibly saved hundreds of lives with an early warning system. This is a plausible story, because it happened again in the flood of 1921.

## DAMAGES

If it is true that a mysterious caller alerted residents to the flooding, this may account for the fact that only two people died in the flood—but two lives lost are two lives too many. Telluride's *Daily Journal* reported the names of the victims as Fred Hill, seventy, and Lydia Bickford, eighty-five. Hill's body was found in the creek the following morning. Bickford had been warned about the flood and refused to leave for higher ground. She died inside her home.

Unfortunately, this is a common response to reports of possible natural disasters. People feel safer in their own homes; even when they are told it is likely they will not survive, they still feel more secure inside their homes and refuse to leave. This also occurred in the Big Thompson Flood disaster of 1976.

Immediately following the flood of 1912, local police reported between twelve and fifteen missing persons as possibly dead, but most of the missing persons were quickly located.

The flood was a shock to the economy, with damage estimates of between $500,000 and $1,000,000. The *Pueblo Chieftain* reported $2,000,000 in damages ($47,698,420 adjusted). One reason the damage estimates were so high was that local merchants stored their stock in warehouses close to the river and creek, where buildings and rent were cheaper. According to Sarah M. Nelson's *Denver: An Archeological History*, the city's west side took the brunt of the financial hit after the flood of 1864 as businesses moved to higher ground and the area experienced a warehouse building boom in the late 1800s. Considering it was the lowest point in the city and already identified as a flood zone, it makes sense that most of the damage in the flood of 1912 was in the warehouse and packinghouse district of West Denver. The city assigned fifteen thousand men to clean up after the flood; most of them were assigned to the warehouse district.

Nelson also discusses the fate of the famous Tremont House Hotel, where the men trapped in the *Commonwealth* newspaper building had sought shelter in the flood of 1864. The building was completely destroyed in the flood of 1912. In the early 1870s, the Tremont was known as the finest hotel in Colorado, but as the years passed and its owners failed to keep up with repairs, the building slowly changed from an upper-class hotel to a boardinghouse and saloon.

The *Denver Republican* described the scene in the Tremont House two days after the flood. Mud and sand reached the top of the bar. The city's cleanup crew made little progress after spending an entire day digging through the

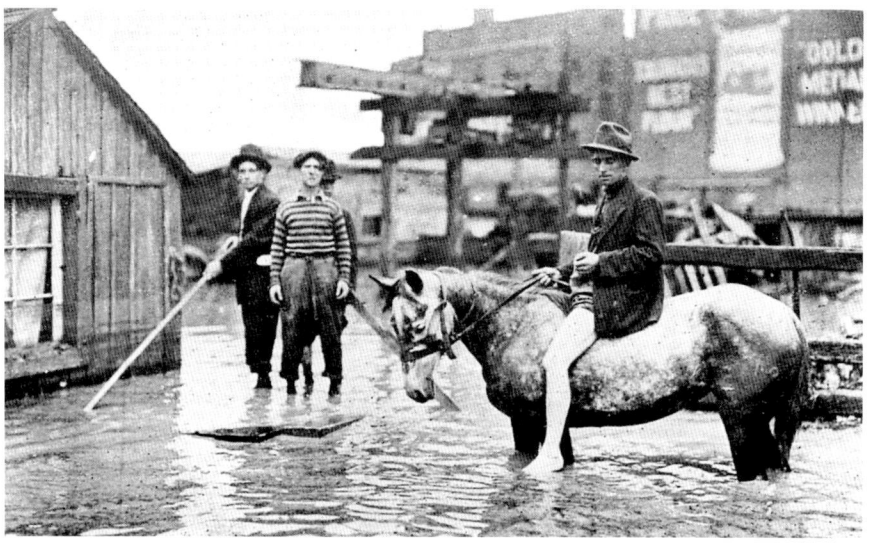

Rescuers at the Bottoms, Denver Flood, July 14, 1912. *29th & Inca Postcard, public domain.*

sludge. The owners of the Tremont were finally told that they had to destroy the building or the fire department would destroy it for them. Nelson also states that Denver's building inspector was forced to condemn between fifty and seventy-five buildings on the banks of both Cherry Creek and the South Platte River.

Most sources state that between five hundred and one thousand residents lost their homes. Denver's mayor ordered temporary housing in the Denver Auditorium (constructed in 1908) for flood victims. The Associate Charities distributed relief funds and rented houses to the homeless. The local telegraph office stated that it broke a record for telegraphs sent by survivors to families and friends. It was considered one of the worst floods to hit Denver, as severe as the flood of 1864. According to Telluride's *Daily Journal*, "The flood is the most terrible that has visited Denver in the history of the city."

## LESSONS LEARNED

After the 1912 disaster, city officials established the 1912 Flood Commission to investigate the floods and recommend steps the city could take for future prevention, including an examination of the Castlewood Dam and the riverfront warehouses.

The instability of the Castlewood Dam had been a concern before the flood, and with good reason. Leaks in the dam were identified prior to the flood; the night of the flood, the water rose so high in the lake behind the dam that it came close to bursting through. The dam continued to be both a concern and a threat to the safety of residents until the day it finally collapsed, bringing even more tragedy to the people of Denver.

# 5
# HEROES ON THE TELEPHONE

## THE PUEBLO FLOOD OF 1921

*If it keeps on raining, levee's going to break*
*If it keeps on raining, levee's going to break*
*When the levee breaks I'll have no place to stay*
*Mean old levee taught me to weep and moan*
*Oh, mean old levee taught me to weep and moan*
*Got what it takes to make a mountain man leave his home.*
—*Blues song composed in 1929 by Kansas Joe McCoy and Memphis Minnie.*
*The song is about the Great Mississippi Flood of 1927, the most destructive river flood in U.S. history.*

The city of Pueblo has a history as colorful and exciting as Denver's. Located on the far south portion of the state, Pueblo is known for its warm winters and rich farmland. Native Americans traveling through the area enjoyed staying at the junction of the Arkansas River and Fountain Creek.

A massacre in 1854, when fifty-four settlers were killed in an attack by the Ute on Christmas Day, seemed to discourage further settlement for a short time, but the beauty of the area continued to draw a wide variety of people, from trappers to Mormons, until 1870, when the settlement became a town in Colorado Territory. General William Jackson Palmer made the first move to plat the town, which he called South Pueblo. His intention was to attract railroad investors, and he succeeded.

Palmer used his knowledge of the area to emphasize a Mexican-American connection and attract investors and workers. In 1881, he financed the construction of a Bessemer furnace south of the river, where the town of Bessemer was eventually platted for workers and businesses. The city now had a steel mill and smelting hub situated on a small bluff with a vast rail yard running along the Arkansas River. The Rockefeller family invested in the city's largest steel mill, the Colorado Fuel and Iron Company.

While North Pueblo became home to railroad and steel mill workers, East Pueblo became the home of the smelter workers. The workers viewed the city as a place to build a home and enjoy life, as opposed to the more oppressive environments of nearby mining towns.

According to Wade Broadhead's *History of Pueblo*, by the late 1890s, Pueblo was possibly the largest city in Colorado, attracting wealthy investors and citizens. These residents invested in extravagant parks with walking paths and exotic landscaping. The late 1800s also brought a building boom of Victorian architecture to the city with large, beautiful mansions.

Unfortunately, many of the poor immigrants lived closer to the railroad tracks and the river so that they could build communities where they remained near their families and friends. The wealthier residents built their homes away from the smell of the mills and the trains, higher on the hillsides. The location of a large community near the river was a disaster waiting to happen.

## THE THREE STORMS OF EARLY JUNE 1921

The first week of June brought the usual unpredictable weather to the area, but the storms that moved through the Arkansas Valley in 1921 left everyone in a state of shock and sorrow.

The flood of 1921 was a three-part disaster. According to the City of Pueblo website, on June 2, a small storm system packed with rain poured into Fountain Creek and the Arkansas River with a terrifying intensity, causing the waters to quickly rise. The rain did not stop. Robert Follansbee, writing for the USGS, reported that the rainfall was so severe that a horse drowned in the rain while standing in a field.

The rain once again increased in intensity on June 3. Mr. E.C. Higgins, whose home was near Canon City Road, later reported seeing heavy cloud cover throughout the day of June 3. A thick layer of black clouds lying on top of the nearby mountain range south of the Arkansas River spread out starting around 1:00 p.m. At about the same time, a similar layer of black clouds sliding across the hilltops near Cripple Creek suddenly seemed to drop low into the valleys. The rain hit the Higgins ranch around 2:00 p.m.

The river and the creek meet in the center of Pueblo. The floodwaters joined. The size of the flood doubled. And the rain continued to fall. Several ranchers reported at least fourteen inches of rain. In the direction of Cripple Creek, the clouds floated low and heavy. Rain fell like thick blankets, obscuring all views of the outside world. Because they were unable to see anything outside of their homes, residents could not make plans for escape and didn't even know if they should try, or if they did, where they would go. The heavy rainfall stole their sense of direction and replaced it with fear. The rain was still heaviest near Pikes Peak, but it was a small matter now—the water was already overflowing the banks. The flood had begun.

The first flood warning started at 6:30 p.m., according to the City of Pueblo. The Pueblo Fire Department had a flood alarm, and flood sirens screamed into the night every fifteen minutes. Residents were told to evacuate from low-lying areas, but a new levee gave the people a false sense

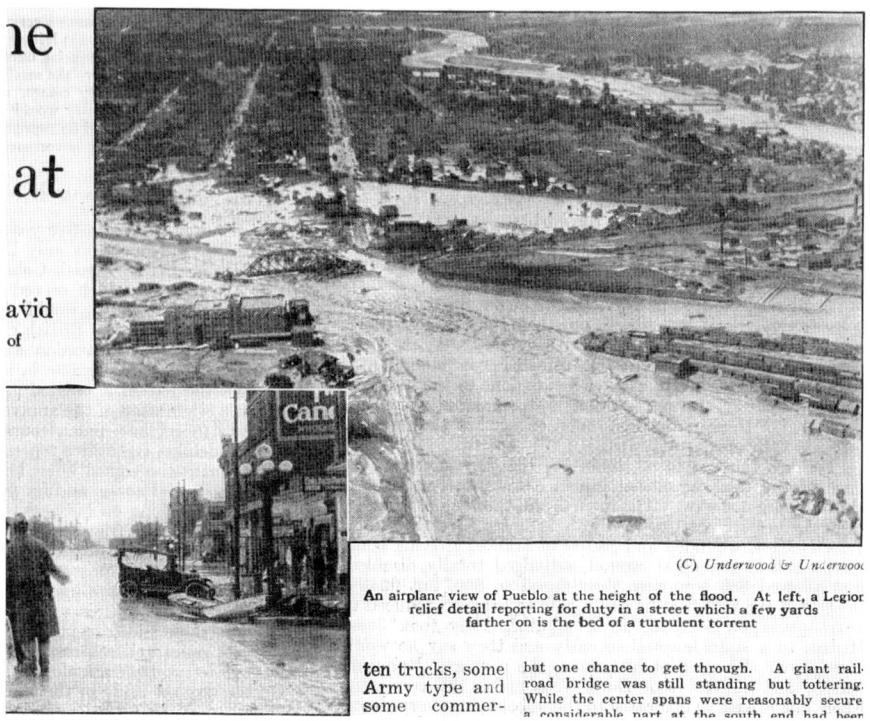

Articles and photos of the Pueblo Flood of 1921 published in the *American Legion Weekly* on July 1, 1921.

of security. Instead of leaving, they crowded onto bridges and around the riverbanks to watch the flood. Soldiers later reported that when they were sent into West Pueblo to enforce the evacuation orders, people fought to remain in their homes. According to the *Colorado Springs Gazette*, one woman, so frightened and desperate to remain near her home, broke away from the soldiers and crawled beneath the house. And the worst was yet to come.

## WHEN THE LEVEES BROKE

At 8:00 p.m. on June 3, the levees collapsed like dominoes. The collapse of the recently improved flood levee created a wall of water and mud at least ten feet high, possibly much higher in places, that slammed into the Union Bridge and across Main Street, taking everything in its path. Trees acted as battering rams against houses and buildings; horses and livestock waiting in pens near the railroad yards drowned and floated belly-up through town. Wade Broadhead stated in his *History of Pueblo* that the strength of the flood was so powerful that it changed the path of the Arkansas River, which now flows a half mile to the south.

An article in the *Fort Collins Courier* told the heartbreaking story of two little girls of the Gray family. Mr. and Mrs. Robert Gray lived near Dry Creek. They heard the floodwaters coming. Mrs. Gray saved four of their children inside the house, where the water was three to four feet deep. Robert Gray was running for the house with eleven-year-old Edna and three-year-old Marjorie when they were struck by the floodwaters from behind. Both girls were ripped from his hands. Robert found safety, but his two daughters drowned. Some of the families near Dry Creek managed to climb to high ground, where they remained stranded for as much as four hours waiting for rescue.

The *Colorado Springs Gazette* told the story of a seventy-five-year-old man who spent the first night clinging to a tree branch. He said he watched at least one hundred people float past him throughout the night. An unidentified witness watched helplessly as over fifty Mexican and Italian families were washed away while trying to escape their community below Union Avenue.

It is believed that at least 260 people died near the railroads alone. The *Plateau Voice* reported that over 100 people were trying to escape on the Fourth Street Bridge when it collapsed, sending everyone into the floodwaters.

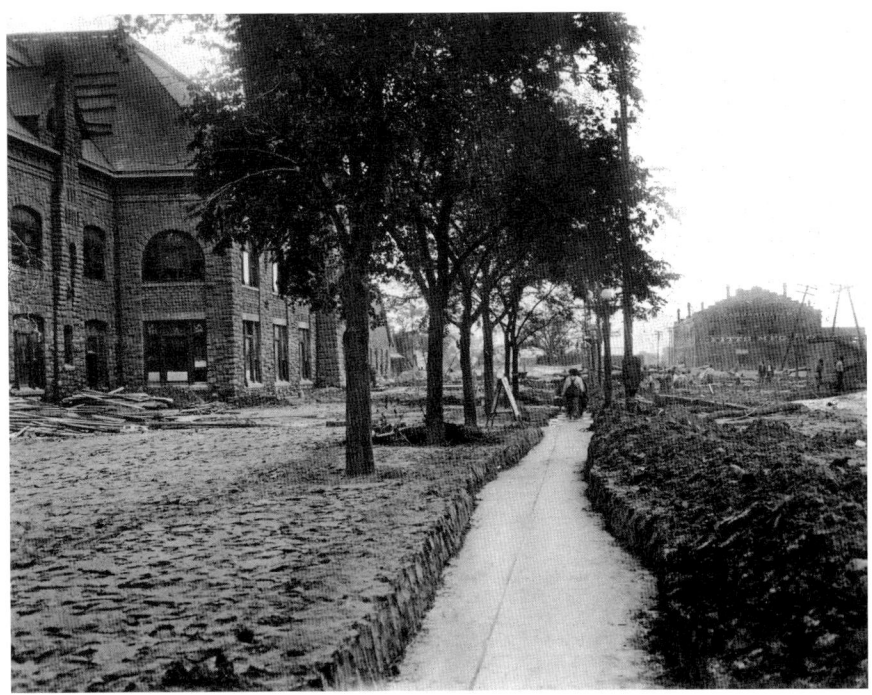

Silt eighteen inches deep deposited in front on Union Depot, Pueblo, Pueblo County, Colorado from the Arkansas River Flood of June 3–5, 1921. Plate 5-A in *U.S. Geological Survey. Water Supply Paper 487, 1922*.

Three bodies were found inside the mangled remains of an overturned Missouri Pacific Train. Rescuers estimated that nearly half of the bodies of the victims would never be found because they were so quickly swept away and buried in the sandbanks. An article posted on the *NOAA* website states that closer to 1,500 people died in the flood of 1921. Most of the bodies were never found, buried beneath the mud and debris. The greatest number of missing and dead were residents of the low-income neighborhoods near the railroads and business districts, as this was lower ground.

## UNION AVENUE'S DISPLAY OF DEATH

The Union Avenue residents were hardest hit. The water moved past buildings and remaining homes with a morbid display of death—the bodies of dead residents mingled with the bloated bodies of horses and cattle, and in between a few floating railcars could be seen. Some of the railcars floated downriver for miles and were never recovered. A fire started in a lumberyard, and burning wood floated among the bodies, adding to the macabre display.

Those who managed to survive did so by climbing to higher ground on Goat Hill. Many residents sought refuge in tall buildings, watching the devastation from the upper floors. The buildings still show the original watermarks from the flood. By the time the water peaked, it was at least fifteen feet high at the intersection of First Street and Santa Fe Avenue, which was also the lowest point of the city according to Broadhead's *History of Pueblo*.

The following morning, Schaeffer Dam collapsed into Beaver Creek, and the city flooded once again. A wild rush of water slammed into passenger trains of the Missouri Pacific and the Denver & Rio Grande. The trains were flipped on their sides as the water swept through the cars, carrying the bodies of victims and their possessions for miles across the local farmlands. More than one hundred people died in the train car disasters. Most of the bodies were torn from the train cars and carried off with the debris and then were buried in the mud and sand downstream.

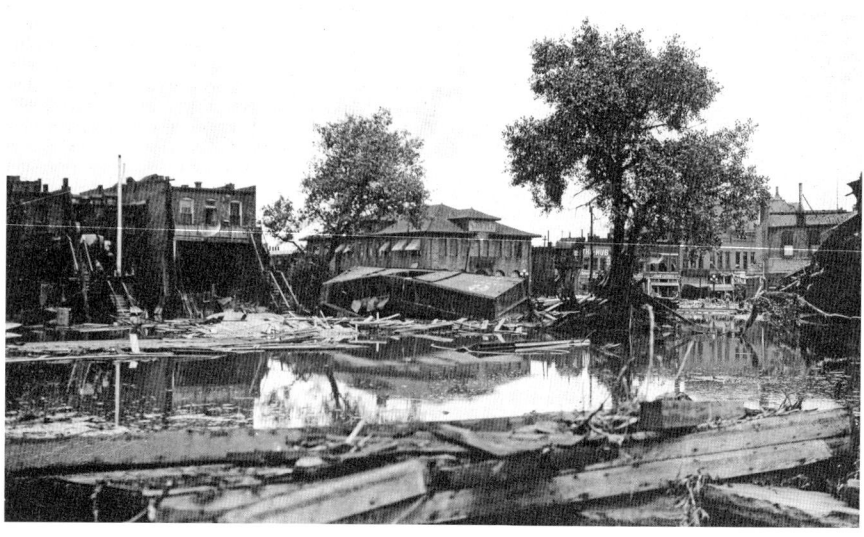

Destroyed buildings and debris amid a large pool of standing water after the flood of 1921 in Pueblo. A note on the back of the photograph reads, "Looking from Main St. into Union Ave." *Courtesy of Pikes Peak Library District, Margaretta M. Boas Photograph Collection.*

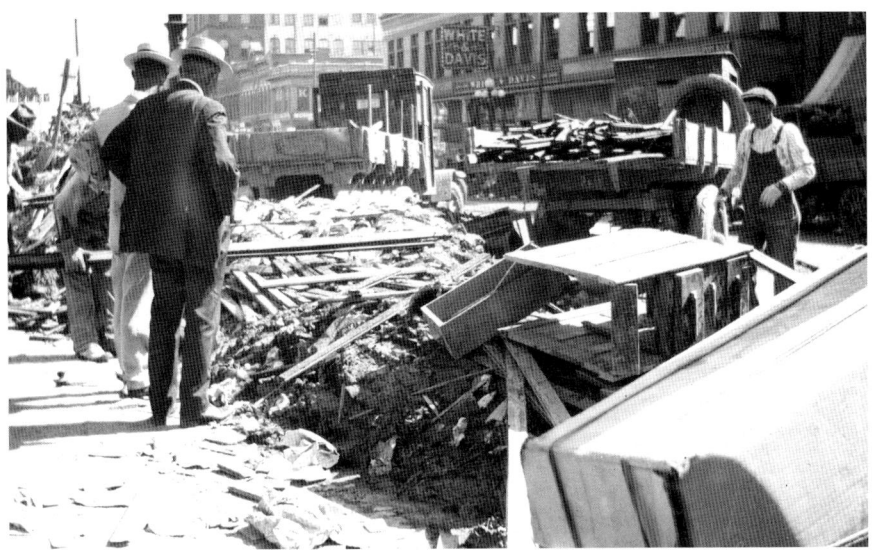

Men staring at debris and building rubble in the center of a street in downtown Pueblo. Trucks hauling off debris are behind. Store signs visible in the background include "White & Davis," "Pope Block" and part of the F.W. Woolworth sign. *Courtesy of Pikes Peak Library District, Margaretta M. Boas Photograph Collection.*

All roads between Colorado Springs and Pueblo were washed away. Charles Dudley, reporter for the *Colorado Springs Gazette*, writing about the flood in 1961, said that one of the most terrifying aspects of the flood was the complete lack of information. One of the local papers, the *Telegraph*, chartered an airplane and sent a reporter to Pueblo in an attempt to provide some sort of information to frantic family members and friends of the people fighting the flood. It sent Ford Frick, who later became the commissioner of Major League Baseball. Frick and the crew flew over Pueblo and saw nothing but water for miles. They couldn't find a place to land close enough to the flood area to give them access to witness reports. Frick took notes on the destruction then returned to Colorado Springs. He stood on top of a soapbox on Pikes Peak Avenue and shouted out the details to a large crowd that had gathered in front of the *Telegraph* office.

The *Colorado Springs Business Journal* reports that two thousand railcars were completely destroyed, eight of the Arkansas and Fountain Creek bridges were critically damaged or completely destroyed and hundreds of buildings were damaged beyond repair. Fires could be seen all across Pueblo. Houses and train cars were drifting through town in the water.

The *Gazette*'s journalist reported hearing hundreds of gunshots fired at looters by soldiers patrolling the flood zones. Two temporary morgues were set up for the 132 bodies recovered within the first hours of the flood.

## ANGELS ON THE TELEPHONE

The first flood warning came from an unknown caller, who telephoned at 6:30 p.m. to report that the Arkansas River was flooding upstream. It is unknown whom the caller was trying to contact—the police, family, perhaps even the operators—but the switchboard operators at Mountain States acted immediately, calling as many people as they could reach and taking calls from those who were desperate and needing comfort.

The Telecommunications History Group has museums in Denver and Seattle, as well as an online resource database. Its Virtual Museum tells a fascinating story about the role of telephones in this disaster. Telephones were the primary means of reaching out to people. They were deliberately used as an early warning system, possibly for the first time in a natural disaster. These pioneers of the telephone warning system truly were "angels." Many of them are not identified by name in sources, but their quick thinking and bravery will always be remembered.

It is miraculous that the telephones worked at all. The City of Pueblo states that all toll lines were destroyed and that seven thousand telephones were out of service. Still, the calls came through, and the company employees did what they could to help.

## THE STORY OF BYRON THADY, TELEPHONE HERO

On the night of the flood, twenty-year-old Byron Thady was one of the operators on duty. He heard the flood siren and ran for the test board to contact Denver. Then the electricity went out, and he knew they were in serious danger. Thady ran for the engine room where he gathered oil cans and rags to make lamps. He continued to make trips throughout the building, searching for supplies to help keep the operators working. When the water reached his waist, a large fire door shut behind him and he was nearly trapped, but he fought his way back out. Thady then ran to the third floor to create a temporary lighting system using the batteries on the second floor.

Mud filled the basement, and the water continued to rise, but the operators stayed at their posts, taking calls, taking names and offering comfort. The terminal room filled with a mix of water and mud up to nine and a half feet, so the operators climbed onto their chairs, using the light from nearby burning buildings to guide them.

Thady and the chief operator, Mrs. Joseph E. Prior, tried to keep the operators from panicking by constant reassurance of the stability of the building. Then they heard cries for help. Thady climbed to a window. He could see a man and a woman on the roof of a nearby structure. He climbed out the window and tried to reach them, to no avail. It is unknown if they were swept away in the flood. Thady told Mrs. Prior in a quiet voice that it was time to move the operators to the third floor. The women who had stood by the telephones all through the night were finally rescued with rowboats the next morning. Thady insisted on staying to connect with the remaining telephones. He continued to work until the following afternoon.

Thady was awarded a Gold Vail Medal and $500 for his actions, but he would probably be the first to say that everyone in the city of Pueblo that night was a hero, from the father who tried desperately to save his children to the operators who stood on chairs when they knew all they could do was offer words of comfort to desperate people. Thady and Mrs. Prior both received distinguished service awards with a statement of recognition for their work:

> DISTINGUISHED SERVICE—PUEBLO FLOOD
> Because of the invaluable service rendered the public, and the unswerving loyalty shown our company during and shortly following the destructive flood at Pueblo, Colorado, June 3, 1921, this tablet of honor is gratefully dedicated to you and to your co-workers who bravely stood the test which none but strong hearts could have endured.
>
> —Ben S. Read, President, The Mountain States Tel. & Tel. Co.

An article on the City of Pueblo website exclaims: "One of the most amazing things about the 1921 flood was not the horrendous amount of damage and life loss, but the bravery and kindness of the people caught in this horrible disaster."

## A SLOW, PAINFUL RECOVERY

An entire city under water for a week—no one could possibly have imagined such chaos. The Elks Club set up a relief center and took in three thousand of the homeless, but it wasn't enough. A camp was established near the Elks Club to house the overflow of people who had lost everything. For an entire week, the people of Pueblo wandered around in a daze, unable to begin recovery work due to the standing water. The smell of rotting animals and unrecovered bodies was unbearable.

When they reached the point at which they felt they couldn't stand one more minute, help finally arrived from the Red Cross, Knights of Columbus, Salvation Army and United States military. The military took control of policing the city to prevent looting and vandalism—Pueblo was under martial law. The Red Cross used huge bonfires to cook food for the homeless and to help keep them warm.

The business district of Union Avenue remained under ten feet of water for over a week. The commercial district was a complete loss. One of the smelters disappeared in the floodwaters. All of the bridges were destroyed. The U.S. Army stayed for six months, doing its best to help restore the city. The business district was slowly moved to Main Street, and Union Avenue remained in a sad state for many years. The survivors undertook three years of hard work to make Pueblo look and operate as a city again, but the total recovery took much longer.

It wasn't until the 1980s that its former productivity returned. The Arkansas River was once again moved to a safer position, and new dams were created. The City of Pueblo also built a Riverwalk to try to attract new residents and tourists. The Riverwalk offers boat rides and sculpture displays along with shopping and dining.

Estimates of the number of flood victims vary, from 78 to 1,500, due to the number of immigrants in the city at the time. Damage to property, businesses and farmland was widespread, stretching from the Arkansas Valley to the Colorado/Kansas border to the east. Property loss was estimated to be $1,096,046,204 (adjusted). At least six hundred homes were destroyed, but the loss of businesses cannot be estimated. In truth, the total loss of life and livestock, as well as damage to businesses, will never be known, due to the fierce, destructive nature of the flood.

## THE STORM OF THE CENTURY

The storm behind the flood of 1912 was fascinating in the way it came upon the area from many different directions then stalled, dumping massive amounts of rain in small places that accumulated into a wall of water. The floodwaters eventually extended thirty miles west of Pueblo and as far as Manitou Springs and Monument Creek in Colorado Springs to the north. There are mountains to the north and south of Pueblo that discouraged the flood from spreading in those directions, but the U.S. Geological Survey reports that observers believed Pikes Peak might have stalled the major contributing storm, causing it to dump massive amounts of rain in a short period of time. It is known that after several days of minor storms there was hard rain on November 3, followed by an intense cloudburst.

There were no weather bureau offices in the area at that time, so rainfall amounts were estimated according to the average water flow; reports of estimated height of the floodwall; the depth of standing water in the city; and estimates of rainfall by area farmers who were familiar with monitoring weather events on their own to predict the damage to crops. According to C.F. Burke, manager of the Blue Ribbon Ranch, the storm came from the northeast and collided with a storm moving from the southwest. This was confirmed by observations from farmer J.H. Farris.

The most destruction from the force of the flood occurred in Pueblo, but the USGS claimed that most of the rain that contributed to the flood fell between Canon City and the city of Pueblo. That same night, there was also flooding on the South Platte River, in Coal Creek, Boulder Creek and St. Vrain Creek, creating damage in Denver and Broomfield. The main body of the flood covered over three hundred square miles.

# 6
# THE 1933 CASTLEWOOD DAM DISASTER

## TELEPHONE OPERATORS SAVE LIVES WHEN DENVER FLOODS

*Know your enemy and know yourself and you can fight
a hundred battles without disaster.*
—Sun Tzu

Some reports claim it rained nonstop for more than a week. Others say it only rained a few days. Regardless of conflicting reports, the fact remained that the ground was completely saturated. The problem was not the number of days it rained, but the amount of rain that fell, saturating the ground until streams were created in the mud flowing toward the irrigation reservoir known as Castlewood Dam. Tiny streams began to form, moving through the forest like fingers of water, creeping toward the reservoir, which was already filling up with rain.

When the many sources of water combined inside the reservoir, the dam collapsed as predicted—the dam had been leaking for many years. It was well known that the design and construction were both flawed. The collapse was disastrous but not a complete surprise. In fact, local residents were prepared and responsive, helping neighbors and strangers and calling to warn others downstream as more than a billion gallons of water crashed down the Cherry Creek toward Denver on August 3, 1933.

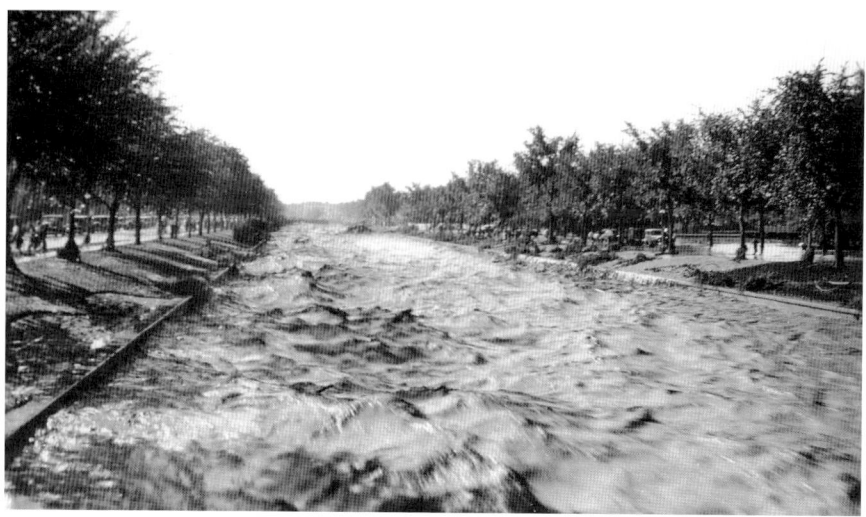

Cherry Creek Flood, August 1933. *CO-L-0006, WaterArchives.org.*

## BUILDING THE CASTLEWOOD DAM

The Castlewood Dam was plagued with controversy since its conception. In spite of all the hard work and money that went into the dam, there were many problems, particularly with the design and the location. The dam was not built to protect Denver from flooding. The dam was created for a group of local residents who wanted to sell large portions of their farmland. These initial investors realized that they needed to offer a reliable water source to sweeten the deal for potential buyers. In order to finance the dam, the landowners, known as the Denver Land and Water Company, partnered with the Denver Water Storage Company. A.M. Welles of Denver was appointed designer and chief engineer.

The dam was located between four and five miles south of Franktown. It was six hundred feet long, seventy feet tall from the floor of the reservoir and eight feet wide along the upper ridge. It had an angled wall and a straight wall, with gravel and concrete used as the support material. The stones used in the construction were taken from the surrounding mountainsides. Newspapers state that the builders hired 85 men to complete the work on the dam; an additional 250 men with 180 horse and mule teams dug the Arapahoe ditch and irrigation canals. The dam, built over an eleven-month period, was completed in 1890.

The former director of Colorado's State Parks Department, George T. O'Malley, and Mrs. Frances Newton recognized the great beauty of the area and decided it needed government protection. They campaigned for funding for the Castlewood Canyon State Park. The construction of the dam and Castlewood Lake attracted even more wildlife to the canyon and surrounding forest, instantly making the area popular with residents of Denver seeking recreation, entertainment and quiet time away from the bustling life of the city.

## DECADES OF CONTROVERSY

Although the park itself was peaceful and quiet, the controversy surrounding the dam was explosive. Rumors circulated that the Denver Land and Water Company was low on funds and unable to sell bonds at the rate it wanted, which naturally made everyone nervous that there would be shortcuts in the construction.

One of the first organizations to voice concerns over the Castlewood Dam was the Flood Commission, established in 1912. The Flood Commission noted that the reservoir was filled with 50 percent silt by the time the dam held any significant amount of water. The commission's studies showed that the dam was in a "serious" state of disrepair and had constant leaks. It was noted that the dam's condition posed potential catastrophic dangers for Denver, but no action was taken.

Shortly after the commission's findings were released, op-ed columns in local newspapers filled with letters from concerned residents. In 1900, chief engineer A.M. Welles, tired of the constant bickering, wrote his own letter in defense of the dam and sent it to the *Denver Post*. Welles said, "The Castlewood dam will never, in the life of any person now living, or in generations to come, break to an extent that will do any great damage either to itself or others."

Welles was not the only corporate executive defending the dam. W.F. Alexander of the Denver Water Storage Company went as far as to imply that complaints and concerns about the Castlewood Dam were voiced out of spite. In a letter posted in the *Denver Times* on May 16, 1891, Alexander said, "If the dam were to be obliterated in an instant and all this water released, the flood would have to travel forty-five miles along the sandy bed of Cherry Creek, which is from one-half to three miles wide, before reaching Denver.…The effect wouldn't be felt at all." The *Rocky Mountain News*, always quick to add its opinion, claimed that the dam actually protected Denver from floods. The local residents formed the opposition. They could see that the dam was already leaking.

On April 11, 1900, the *Denver Times* reported that the dam would undergo a thorough inspection. Then, mysteriously, ten days later, representatives from the City of Denver stated that there would be no inspection—the dam was already deemed safe. The city's safety statement inflamed critics who continued to argue via letters to the editors of local newspapers about the dangers already present at the dam. The bottom line was that the dam did provide water necessary for local farm operations, for everything from potatoes to sugar beets—and money trumped safety.

Risking his reputation and employment, one assistant city engineer, Andrew Ryan, made his own public statement regarding the safety of the dam: "I do not want to say anything that will hurt the company and I do not want to frighten the people along the creek, but everything is not as I should like to see it." Ryan made his statement just days after the city claimed the dam was secure.

## NEW OWNERS AND A SERIES OF BANKRUPTCIES

The Denver Water Storage Company filed for bankruptcy in 1901. Its assets, including the Castlewood Dam, went to the creditor owed the most, the Knickerbocker Investment Company of New York.

According to *The Night the Dam Gave Way: A Diary of Personal Accounts*, it was only three years later that the dam changed hands again. The new owners, the Denver Suburban Homes and Water Company, decided to return the dam to its original purpose, serving local farmers. From 1904 to 1912, the dam provided irrigation water to orchards and alfalfa fields. Then the company devised a plan to plant cherry trees and sell small land plots perfect for retirement couples. The plan looked good on paper, but potential investors were not easily convinced, and this company was also forced to file bankruptcy.

For more than ten years, the water in the reservoir and its potential for farm irrigation were subjects of numerous lawsuits. Ironically, the lovely cherry tree orchards died from lack of water in spite of the fact that billions of gallons of water were readily available. At one time, the water from the reservoir was used to irrigate 2,500 acres of fruit orchards, alfalfa fields and other crops.

Ownership of the dam was transferred to eight different companies. Finally, in 1923, the landowners decided to purchase the water rights; management of the dam went to 150 farmers and ranchers who formed the Cherry Creek Mutual Irrigation Company. But the safety issues were not forgotten. Every time the dam changed hands, the new owners or committees of owners hired engineers and filed reports, studies and photos insisting the dam was safe.

In spite of the studies, the dam had visible cracks and continued to leak. In fact, the safety of the dam was debated by various government agencies from the day it was completed to the day it finally collapsed in 1933.

## ALL IT TAKES IS A CLOUDBURST...

The Castlewood Dam collapsed on August 3, 1933, because of a cloudburst. The storm poured rain into the Cherry Creek drainage basin for several days, and residents reported that rain in some areas lasted as long as a week. Eight inches of rain fell in just three hours on August 2.

It was a terrifying sight. The clouds were black, and the sky was dark even at midday. Lightning crashed constantly throughout the canyon. As with most cloudbursts, the rain fell in sheets.

By midnight, the rainwater reached the top of Castlewood Dam. Fifteen minutes later, the water was pouring through and over the dam. The forty-three-year-old structure finally collapsed, sending billions of gallons of water racing through the canyon. It was the beginning of a thirty-five-mile rampage down the mountain to Denver.

## RESCUED BY TELEPHONE

The dam's caretaker, Hugh Paine, lived near the facility with his wife. Paine spoke with reporters from the *Rocky Mountain News* the day after the flood, and his account of the dam break is also recorded in *The Night the Dam Gave Way*. Paine and his wife listened to the rolling thunder for hours, discussing the condition of the dam. Around 1:00 a.m., they decided to try

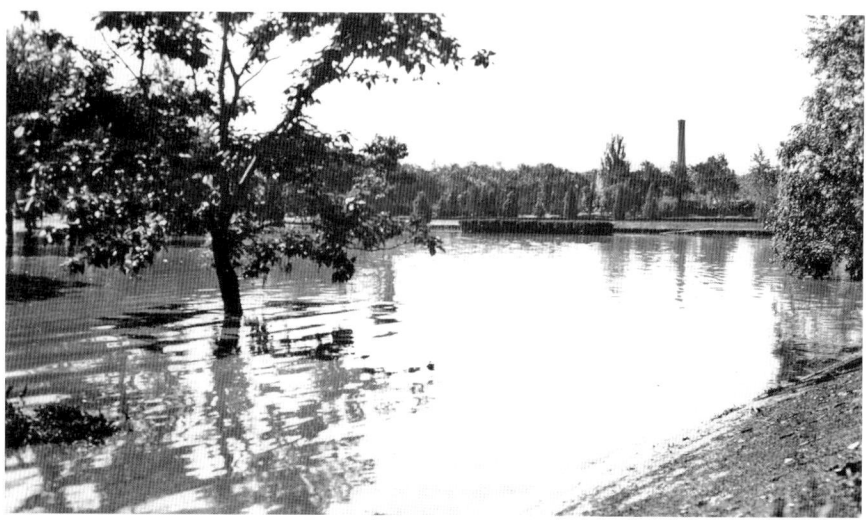

Cherry Creek Flood, August 1933. *CO-L-0007, WaterArchives.org.*

to get some sleep, then they heard the crash of the dam and the booming sounds of a flash flood.

Paine's wife watched in terror through the windows of their house while her husband searched for a lantern. The flood was already on its path, carrying trees and boulders down the mountain. Paine's telephone line was no longer working. He had to run in the dark to the home of a neighbor, Ed Hall. They walked twelve miles in the rain and slippery mud around the back of the lake before reaching a phone at Castle Rock, where they were able to call the Denver police and the Parker telephone operators, Mr. and Mrs. August Deepe.

## NETTIE DRISKILL HARTH

Farmers, ranchers and homeowners in the flood's path shared party lines at that time. Residents were notified of a call to their homes by individual codes, a series of short and long rings assigned to their homes by the telephone company. The emergency code was universal—one long ring. Homeowners answered the call for information on the type of emergency. In 1933, it was a flood, and the instructions shouted into the phone were to run for high ground.

Nettie Driskill Harth lived in the Deepe home and worked as a phone operator for ten dollars an hour plus room and board. Harth told her story in *The Night the Dam Gave Way*. When August Deepe told Harth that the flood was coming, she ran for the switchboard and called as many people as she could.

Harth knew that people were heading for the local bridge to watch the flood, but Mrs. Deepe told residents to run for their lives. Harth didn't know how severe the flood was and didn't know if she was in danger, but she refused to leave her post, calling everyone on the subscriber list, urging them to run for high ground.

After the flood, Harth was told that she was considered a hero to the residents of Parker. She was interviewed by *Time* magazine and the *Denver Post*.

## THE SHERIFF AND THE DISPATCHERS

Meanwhile, one of Colorado's many unknown heroes, a Douglas County sheriff, managed to sound the flood alarm from Franktown. The sheriff realized he couldn't possibly reach the many homes in the path of the flood. His quick thinking in an emergency situation sent him in search of a telephone. He notified the Sullivan Telephone Exchange, located in the living room of the home of Elsie Henderson.

Telephone operator Elsie Henderson was on duty and took the call. The sheriff's instructions were detailed and precise—farmers and ranchers along Cherry Creek must be called immediately so they could move cattle, horses and other livestock away from the water's edge. They were also told to take their families to high ground. The sheriff then instructed Henderson to contact Mountain States Telephone Company so that its operators could contact Denver's police, fire departments, radio stations and as many residents as possible.

Henderson was joined by coworker Ingrid Mosher, and the two women worked at a feverish pace, following the sheriff's instructions and sending out the long ring on the wires, desperately trying to reach as many residents as possible before the water reached the farms, ranches and homes. Some accounts also state that Fay Davis assisted with the calls. The women remained at their dispatch stations throughout the night and into the following morning. They were finally relieved of their posts in the afternoon hours of August 3.

It is estimated that five thousand people were saved through this early warning system—that was the number of homes evacuated after receiving emergency notification calls from Henderson and Mosher. The displaced residents were temporarily sheltered in local hotels.

## ONE HALF BILLION GALLONS OF WATER

The day after the flood, the *Denver Post* reported that the first calls reached Denver around 2:38 a.m. Residents were told that a fifteen-foot wall of water was about to hit the city. By 4:00 a.m., every police car and fire truck in Denver was racing through the city, searching for families that didn't receive the call and rescuing those who received the call too late. One man was on the streets when the floods came and saved himself by climbing a telephone pole.

Dwight D. Gross, chief engineer for the Denver Board of Water Commissioners, stated that the flood was reduced to around 500,000,000 gallons of water by the time it reached Denver, but the flood was carrying

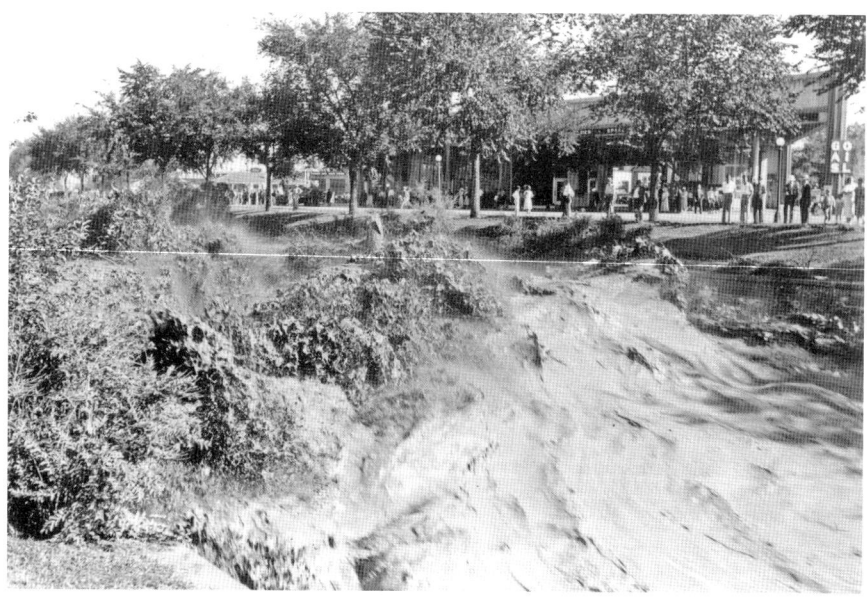

View of a Cherry Creek flood in Denver, Colorado, after the Castlewood Canyon Dam break. Shown are torrents of muddy water in standing waves at Acoma Street. People watch from under trees. *Photo by Charles E. Eyser, courtesy of the Denver Public Library.*

# Colorado's Deadliest Floods

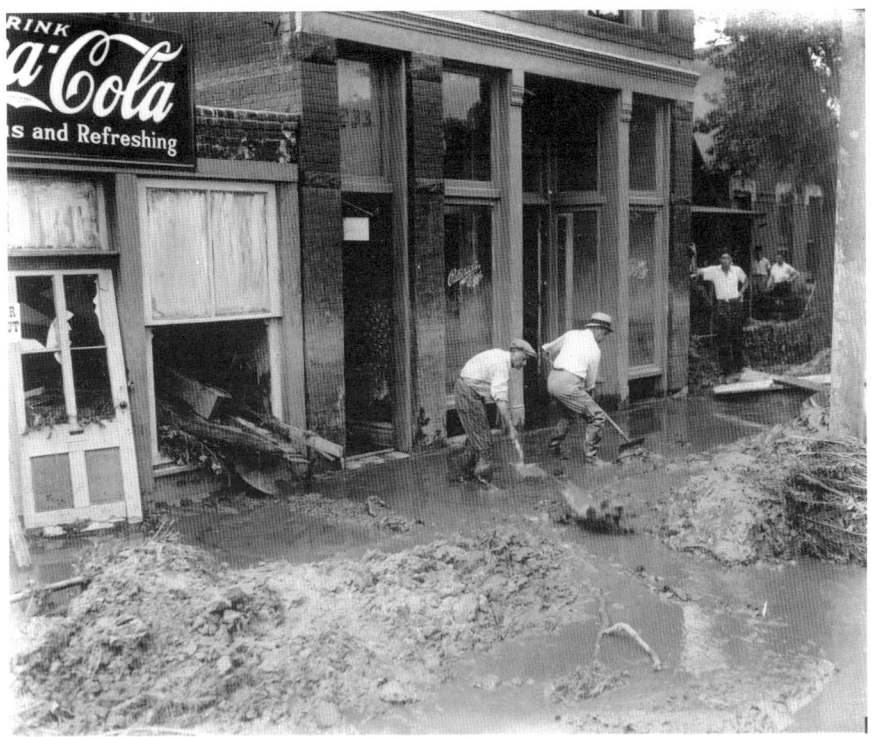

Cherry Creek Flood damage, Castlewood Dam disaster, August 1933. Men use shovels to clear mud from the flood after the Castlewood Canyon Dam break in Denver, Colorado. Teenage boys look on. Storefront signs read, "Coca Cola," "Patterson's Eggs" and "233." *Denver News photo, courtesy of the Denver Public Library.*

twenty thousand tons of dirt and debris left behind in the city after the water moved on six hours later. A film made of the flood in 1933, which is now at the Denver Public Library, shows houses collapsing and breaking apart in the floodwater while people watch from the newly formed riverbanks.

The film also shows crowds of people standing on the bridges watching the water in spite of the obvious danger. They were watching horses and other animals trapped beneath the bridge. The animals were tangled in the debris, which was building up beneath the bridge, creating another potential threat to residents. According to George W. Madsen, whose story is told in *The Night the Dam Gave Way*, policemen and ranchers with rifles were seen at the bridges, telling the people to leave and move to higher ground. The ranchers then went to the water's edge. They seemed uncomfortable, particularly with all the children watching, but their job was to shoot the horses and other animals drowning in the flood so the bodies could be cleared with the debris and the dam could be saved.

The Castlewood Dam break sent floodwaters into Castlewood Park, Franktown, Parker, Denver, Cherry Creek Valley and surrounding areas. A team of 2,500 men was hired to help rebuild destroyed bridges and buildings. Although one source reported that two campers died in the flood, it was later determined that this was untrue. Tom Casey, eighty-three, died when he returned to his home to retrieve his property. Bertha Caitlin, twenty-four, from Kansas, died when she rode her horse near the floodwaters to survey the damage. Her horse panicked and threw her into the flood.

The total damage is estimated at $1.7 million ($30 million today). Castlewood Dam was not repaired or rebuilt. Instead, the City of Denver built Cherry Creek Dam in 1946.

# 7
# MIRACLES AND TRAGEDIES

## THE MONUMENT CREEK AND KIOWA CREEK FLOODS OF 1935

*One does not appreciate the sight of earth until he has traveled through a flood. At sea one does not expect or look for it, but here, with fluttering leaves, shadowy forest aisles, housetops barely visible, it is expected. In fact a graveyard, if the mounds were above water, would be appreciated.*
—Anonymous, New Orleans Times-Democrat, *March 29, 1882*

When survivors talk about the floods of 1935, it's what they don't say that is shocking. They don't talk about houses filled with mud, the removal of water from basements or lost possessions. They talk about their home slowly moving off its foundation then floating down the river with family members still clinging to the roof; they talk about watching houses split in half then slam into a bridge or sink in the water; they talk about watching the homes of their neighbors explode in a cloud of dust and debris.

In flood situations, observers often state that they didn't think the rain would ever stop. In some situations, that appears to be true. On May 30, 1935, 24 inches of rain fell in six hours at two locations in eastern Colorado, 22.8 inches in four hours alone. The rain came from a massive storm system that covered the borders of Colorado, Nebraska and Kansas along the path of the drainage basin. It was as if the storm had a mind of its own, as if it was an intelligent storm, moving with precision and skill. It was powerful, deadly and strange. The rainfall locations were five hours apart, the first near Burlington and the second near Colorado Springs. The first storm started around noon and ended at 6:00 p.m.; the second started at 7:00 p.m., an hour after the first one ended, and ended at 3:00 a.m. the next morning.

There was a third rain gauge stationed between these two locations. It registered eleven inches of rainfall between 6:00 p.m. and 9:00 p.m. Another gauge in Seibert registered nine inches of rain in two hours. In each instance, the rain fell on flat terrain in areas that generally receive an average of sixteen inches of rain over the span of an entire year. According to a report by the Department of Army Corps of Engineers, the fact that so much rain was recorded by four separate gauges is enough evidence that the rain records are accurate. The report stated that the rainfall on May 30, 1935, was the most "ever recorded anywhere on earth."

On that date, eastern Colorado experienced a cloudburst, the strength of which had never been seen before. Robert Follansbee, writing for the United States Geological Survey, provided a detailed definition for Colorado cloudbursts and their severity: "Cloudbursts occur only where there is a marked range in temperature within a relatively small area. This condition exists chiefly in the Foothills, where the warm air from the plains drifts toward the mountains, is deflected upward, and cools rapidly at the higher altitudes near the heads of the canyons. For this reason cloudbursts generally occur in the afternoon or early evening of an unusually warm day. On rare occasions rainfall of cloudburst intensity occurs as far east as the eastern edge of the State." Follansbee lists examples of Colorado residents caught in cloudbursts experiencing symptoms similar to that of drowning and a horse that was drowned by the rain while it stood in a field.

There was more than one storm, more than one cloudburst, more than one flood. There was flooding in Kiowa, in Colorado Springs, in surrounding areas and in Nebraska and Kansas from the same storm system. The event was severe, dangerous and deadly. In the end, a large portion of the state of Colorado was under water. All three states mourned victims of the floods. Traumatized survivors fought to piece their lives back together.

## CHOCOLATE CLOUDS

This was so much more than a severe storm; this was extreme rain. At first, it was a source of fascination, rain so hard and fast it hurt the skin. After a few hours, the rain became a serious source of concern. When the deluge began to ease, after six hours and twenty-four inches of rain, the people of eastern

Colorado were already running for high ground to escape the floods. But this flood happened on the plains, and there was no high ground.

The clouds were full and heavy in a storm that could be seen for miles before it actually arrived. When it did finally arrive, the children were already inside, staring out the windows, shivering with fear. The clouds and rain made it feel like nighttime during daylight hours.

In a report republished on the website Weather Underground, Colorado's Weather Bureau Climatological Data for that day noted an interesting phenomenon: coppery brown clouds. Residents observing the storms from the distance did not see the typical black clouds one would expect from a storm of this magnitude, which is why the children were home. Their parents had seen the storm coming, realized it was no ordinary storm and ran for the schools. There was something in the clouds that frightened them. The clouds were fierce, threatening and a copper/chocolate-brown color.

In an odd coincidence, according to Meteorologist Mike Nelson's *Colorado Weather Almanac*, the year before the great flood, 1934, was the "hottest and driest year in Colorado's history until the drought that began in the late 1990s." The 1930s are known as the years of the Dust Bowl when drought and strong winds ruled the weather in the United States spurring a mass migration as Americans lost their homes and farms and searched for a better life. The massive dust storms played a part in the mystery and the creation of the flood of 1935, as well as an explanation for the chocolate-brown clouds.

The chocolate brown clouds were a combination of events including a massive dust storm on the Colorado/Kansas border. This storm was high and wide and could be seen from miles away. As the rainstorm raged nearby with intervals of deadly baseball-sized hail, the sky took on a copper chocolate color. According to the weather bureau, the clouds "cast a brown shadow, giving the scene a weird appearance."

The frequent dust storms also covered and smothered the vegetation in the area, killing plant roots that could have helped hold at least some of the rain. As it was, the rain fell on mounds of dust and rolled off toward the rivers. The dust storm continued after the floodwaters receded. Searchers were forced to fight the dust as they searched the mud for victims of the flood, creating a surreal, macabre environment that survivors would never forget.

## COLORADO SPRINGS

May 1935 was a rainy month for Colorado Springs. In fact, that month saw the most rain in the forty-eight-year history of rainfall record keeping in Colorado, according to the USGS. That season was in stark contrast to the hot, dry weather of the previous year. By the end of May, the ground was completely saturated. On May 28 and 29, the city experienced light but continuous showers, adding to the saturation problem. By May 30, the rain was a steady downpour.

Early in the afternoon, black clouds appeared on the horizon moving down from the north. A series of cloudbursts hit Colorado Springs, then stalled at almost precisely the same time that a massive storm battered the eastern portion of the state—the distance between Kiowa and Colorado Springs is a one-hour drive, or forty-eight miles.

Residents of Colorado Springs had planned a Memorial Day Parade for May 30, but when they woke up that morning, a thick fog covered the city and the rain continued to fall. According to the *Colorado Springs Gazette*, only fourteen veterans arrived to march in the parade because it was too wet and muddy for a march. The sky grew darker by the hour.

The water in Monument Creek, which flows into Colorado Springs and meets up with Fountain Creek, rose phenomenally fast. In 2011, Pulitzer Prize–winning reporter Dave Philips wrote about the 1935 flood for the *Gazette* using articles from the former *Colorado Springs Gazette*. According to Philips, the *Colorado Springs Gazette* had witness reports of "hail drifts eight feet high." Then millions of gallons of floodwater barreled into the city with a floodwall of unbelievable height, tearing trees out by their roots and smashing homes into splinters. Dozens of homes were moved from their foundations or simply crushed by the force of the water.

There were so many trees in the water that they looked like battering rams slamming into the city in a great battle. The flood was one quarter of a mile wide at Monument Valley Park. This flood had more than a "wall of water," according to the *Colorado Springs Gazette*. The water moved so fast and hard that it pushed against the debris and shot ten to fifteen feet into the air.

Stunned survivors watched in horror as a barn filled with hay was smashed into tiny pieces. The scene became even more surreal when the flood hit a carnival set up near the riverbanks. The Ferris wheel toppled on its side, and carnival rides were picked up by the water and bounced around on the waves as if they were the passengers in a deadly holiday celebration.

# Colorado's Deadliest Floods

The Mesa Road Bridge crumbled against the onslaught of the battering trees. The Rock Island Railroad bridge was already in pieces. The Nevada Avenue Bridge, which was reinforced with concrete, "snapped like cardboard" according to one witness speaking to a *Colorado Springs Gazette* reporter. By the time the flood had spread to a mile wide, it had savagely obliterated every bridge in town but one, the Bijou Street Viaduct. By the end of the day, every road in the city, as well as the city's train tracks, was destroyed. Then the flood hit the power plant, and the already darkened city turned as black as the clouds. Communication and transportation were impossible. With no light for guidance, the people of the city were caught in the deluge.

The *Colorado Springs Gazette* tells of a man trapped in muddy water up to his neck. He was working at the grocery store on Colorado Avenue when the flood hit. He waited for hours in the freezing water before he was rescued.

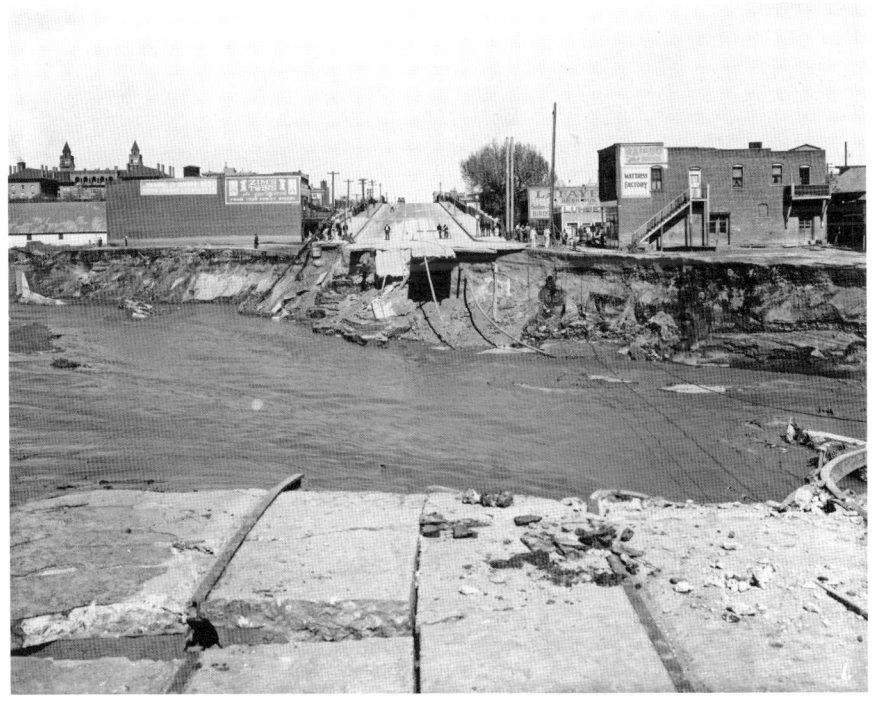

Washed out road at Colorado Avenue. People are standing on the far side of the creek surveying damage. May 1935. *Courtesy of Pikes Peak Library District, Stewarts Commercial Photographers Collection.*

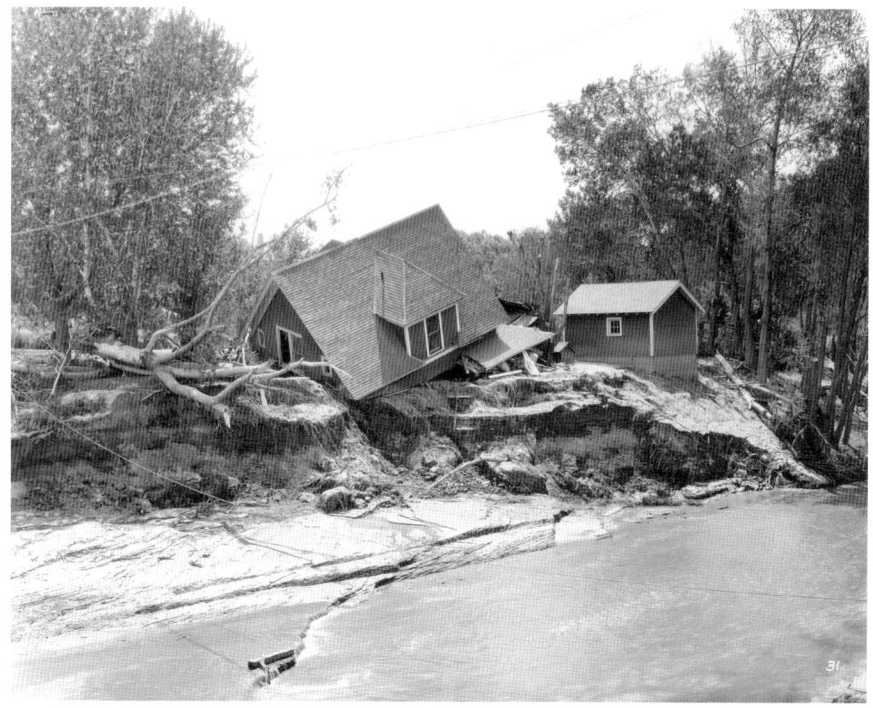

Badly damaged house, identified on back as the home of park superintendent Gustav A. Hennenhofer. Also seen is the site of Uintah Street Bridge, showing damage caused by the Memorial Day flood in 1935. *Courtesy of Pikes Peak Library District, Stewarts Commercial Photographers Collection.*

Another resident, T.J. Fagan, helped his family to high ground and then returned to his home to retrieve some of their belongings. Fagan was caught by the flood and carried seventy-five feet downstream before his son was able to grab him and drag him onto a submerged car. The two men waited on top of the car for hours before they were rescued.

The *Colorado Springs Business Journal* tells the story of an unnamed man who ran to a gas station for shelter when the floodwall hit. He was carried along in the water, screaming for help. Suddenly, the man felt a log slam up against him. He grabbed onto the log and threw his body over the top. He rode the log all the way to Fountain, Colorado, before it collided with a debris jam and he was able to climb to safety.

## THAT HELPLESS, HOPELESS FEELING

There was one story reported by all of the newspapers, one story so tragic that it tore at the hearts of everyone in the city. A young couple from Pueblo was driving through town when their car was caught in the floodwaters. The young man climbed onto the top of the car, shouting for help as he assisted the young woman climbing out the window. The man was wearing a stylish black suit. The woman was dressed in white. Witnesses commented on her lovely, blond hair.

Who were they, and where were they going on that rainy afternoon? Did the young man see the flood coming when it was still three feet deep and think he could drive through it? Did he, confused by the water and the rain, take a deadly turn and drive into the river? The couple was dressed in black and white—was this their wedding day? A few small towns had plans for high school graduations. Were they meeting family? What did they think as they were clinging to each other in the cold and rain? They could see the men trying to help them. They could see the ever-growing crowd above. What did they say in their last moments?

Eventually, a crowd of thousands had gathered on the banks to watch the flood. They crowded on a hilltop near the car to watch, and the couple watched them. Some of the people on the banks were taking photographs of the couple as the man and the woman stared back in shock. Volunteer rescuers ran to the water's edge, groups of men trying to find a way to reach the couple, shouting instructions, searching for branches, rope, anything that might help bring the couple closer to the river's ever-widening banks.

At first, the crowd shouted their encouragement, but time moves quickly for people who are trapped by a flood. As the crowd watched huge trees rushing past the car, animals struggling in the water and large sections of homes whipping past the car and barely missing the young couple, the people on the banks gradually began to talk in whispers, or not at all. The men on the edge of the river refused to give up hope. They continued to search for ways to rescue the young couple, and the water continued to rise until it flowed wildly over the delicate white shoes of the young woman.

Moments later, the crowd was silent. They knew in their hearts what was about to come. They could see the wall of water racing toward the car. The car leapt forward, then went beneath the muddy water, dragging the screaming couple beneath the debris. The men on the riverbanks, the rescue team, ran as quickly as they could, shouting for the couple, begging them to rise once more from the waters so they could try one more time to save them, but the man and the woman simply disappeared. Days later, their bodies were found buried in the mud miles away from where the horrific scene took place. Their story and their names are lost to time, but the memory of what happened will never be forgotten.

## ELBERT'S MEMORIAL/GRADUATION DAY

The month of May was a wet one for Elbert County. The ground was saturated, and the rain continued to fall, interspersed with brief, furious hailstorms. Tiny rivulets began to form in the mud and grass. Most of the homes at that time were built on the sides of the hills, but there were a few structures on the riverbanks.

It didn't matter where the homes were in Elbert, because the flood occurred in the middle of the day and the residents of Elbert were out on the roads and sidewalks when the river began to flood around 9:00 a.m. There would be no Memorial Day celebration in the town of Elbert. There would be no graduation. The school was destroyed.

Elbert had two floods on May 31. The first struck the town at 9:00 a.m. as the people were leaving their homes to start their day. Mud and water filled the streets and fields as far as the residents could see, but they thought this was the last of their troubles for the morning.

Then, around noon, a second flood struck the town. According to Burton Eisner, who told his story for the National Oceanic and Atmospheric Administration (NOAA) website, the second flood had a water wall between ten and fifteen feet high "with the speed of a horse" that caught everyone in town completely off guard. Houses didn't move or break apart, they exploded. Along with the homes, the floods destroyed a pool hall, shoe shop, newspaper office and numerous other businesses, a total of fifty buildings.

There was no official measurement of water height or flow in Elbert, but survivors estimate a water wall of between eight and fifteen feet. The water killed nine people. After the flood moved on, it left behind five feet of sand from the nearby sandstorm. All of Elbert's bridges were washed away. In fact, three quarters of the town was completely destroyed, and these sections were never rebuilt. Many buildings were erected on the sides of hills and not damaged.

## KIOWA

Kiowa began in the mid-1800s as a stop for Butterfield Overland and Wells Fargo stagecoaches headed for Denver. It is the county seat of Elbert County and a four- to five-hour drive northeast of Colorado Springs—but much faster for floodwater.

In addition to Memorial Day gatherings, residents in Kiowa were planning to celebrate graduation for the Elbert High School class of 1935. The ceremony never took place. After the floods hit Elbert, the water moved on to Kiowa. According to a USGS study, the primary source of the flooding in and around Kiowa was Kiowa and Bijou Creeks, which flow into the South Platte River. There is some confusion as to when and where flooding started on Kiowa Creek, but Bijou Creek rose to flood level at 11:30 p.m. on May 30 and again on May 31 at 3:30 a.m.

The flood struck like a mighty fist, slamming into homes and businesses. The initial water wall destroyed two creameries, the city garage and several homes. According to the story of Burton Eisner, retold on the NOAA website, a young mother and her baby were washed away in the flood while her remaining children watched from the branches of a tree. Many local farmers lost their crops, which were covered in sand. They also lost their livestock and homes.

The peak of the flood reached Fort Morgan at 5:30 a.m. with a height ten feet above normal, then rapidly dropped back down. Water flowed everywhere—upstream, downstream, all across the land—and this reduced the height of the floodwall. It was highest at Fort Morgan. A Union Pacific Railroad grade twenty-five miles downstream of Sterling collapsed, and the river created a half-mile-wide lake north of Highway 19 with a floodwall of fifteen feet.

## AND WHEN THE RAIN WAS OVER...

After the flood, the Red Cross arrived to help with housing, food and clothing, and the National Guard arrived to help with cleanup and to prevent looting. The railroad companies decided not to repair the damaged tracks, which prevented Fort Morgan and Sterling from making a complete recovery.

Determining an estimate of loss is difficult due to record-keeping practices of the time and the vastness of the flood, which occurred over three states. Colorado and Nebraska were almost equally devastated; tragic stories from the Nebraska flooding will never be forgotten.

The number of victims of the floods varies widely. According to Christopher Burt, writing for Weather Underground, approximately 113 people were killed; 41,500 cattle were reported missing or dead. In addition, 341 miles of highway, 307 bridges and 74,500 acres of farmland and crops were destroyed. The damage to railroads was impossible to pinpoint, but a total damage estimate comes to $800 million adjusted.

# 8
# THE 1965 COLORADO FLOODS

## CATASTROPHIC FLOODING IN THE SOUTH PLATTE AND ARKANSAS RIVER BASINS

*The Facts of Life and Death Remain the Same. We live and die, we love and grieve, we breed and disappear. And in between those existential gravities, we search for meaning, save our memories, leave a record for those who will remember us.*
—*Thomas Lynch*

Is it possible to escape a flood that covers the largest city in the state? Dams break, bridges fall, roads crack and homes and families completely disappear in the dark, swirling waters. This is what happened when the big floods swarmed across Colorado in 1965.

Widespread rain, a result of cloudbursts, spread throughout the state from June 14 to 18. Most of the rain fell south of Denver. The water moved to the South Platter River, which flows through Denver. The South Platte, Cherry Creek and all of their tributaries flooded. The storms and resulting floods began near Pueblo, where residents were evacuated from their homes, and Granada, where residents were also evacuated. The storms marched on to Colorado Springs, where they grew in strength, then to Monument, smashing into Denver, Loveland, Fort Collins, Greeley, Sterling and everywhere in between before moving on to Nebraska. Tornadoes touched down in Fountain, Castle Rock and farther north in Loveland, where Linda Rae Beeman Rein, thirteen, was killed when she was swept into Buckhorn Creek by the water overflowing its banks.

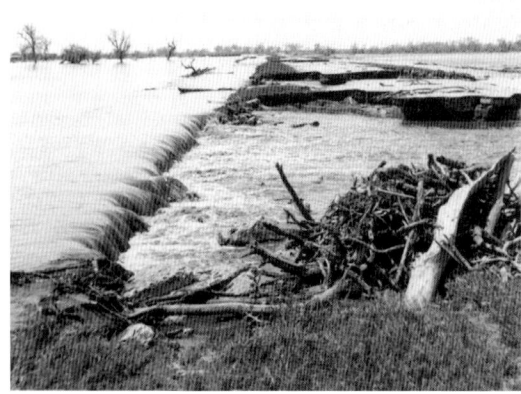

Flooding on the South Platte River in 1965. *Courtesy of Colorado Department of Natural Resources.*

Hail the size of golf balls and baseballs fell hard and fast across the state. Crops were smashed in the fields and livestock killed where they stood. Those animals that did manage to survive the storms were killed in the floods. According to the *Colorado Tribune*, the pilot of a small plane lost control of the craft in the storm and was killed in a crash near Byers.

By this time, residents were beginning to see a pattern. Mike Nelson explains in his *Colorado Weather Almanac* that the floods were created by a deep, upper-level storm system hanging over the American West that "made the atmosphere unstable." Powerful thunderstorms poured rain on the cities for days, saturating the ground until tiny rivulets began to flow through the mud toward the rivers. The South Platte River eventually crested at twenty-five feet above its normal level.

But the storms didn't isolate themselves over Denver. They marched along the Foothills in a line, then spread east. The floods followed close behind, and when they arrived, they were like a nightmare, a repeat of the same catastrophic flooding that had occurred thirty years earlier, in 1935. And it would happen again in 2013.

## SOUTHERN COLORADO

The storms preceding the floods in southern Colorado were tremendous. In Colorado Springs, hail the size of golf balls piled up in the streets. Soldiers from Fort Carson were using shovels to dig hail out of basements. In that city, winds reached sixty-three miles per hour and knocked out all telephone service.

As the flood spread south into Colorado Springs, it was still so deep that it reached the upper edges of the Uintah Street Bridge on Monument Creek. Moving through Fountain Creek, the flood continued to smash roads and shatter bridges. In the southern portion of Colorado, an additional one million acres of farmland were destroyed.

The town of Holly received enough notice to evacuate, and eleven railroad boxcars lined up on the south side of town helped prevent the town from completely washing away.

The Arkansas River raged on, crashing into the levee on the west side of Granada until it crumbled. According to Gregory D. Everhart, writing for the U.S. Army Corp of Engineers Albuquerque Division, the residents of Granada knew the flood was coming and were sandbagging the west side of town when the floodwaters struck. Everhart and his brother worked at the local movie theater while their father helped with sandbagging. Their mother arrived to take them home around 11:30 p.m.; as soon as they

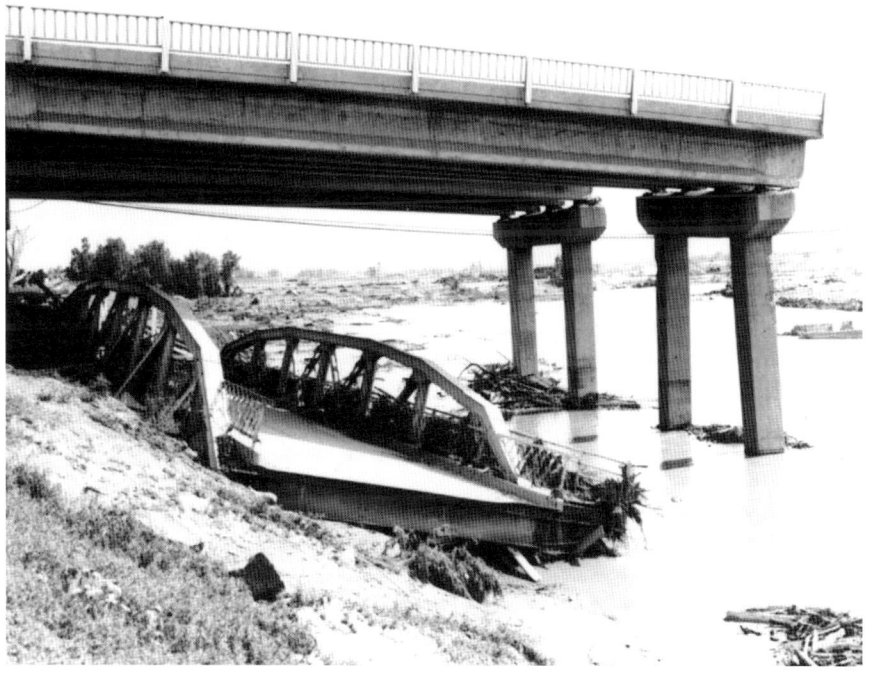

Bridge damage from the 1965 flood on the South Platte River. *Courtesy of Colorado Department of Natural Resources.*

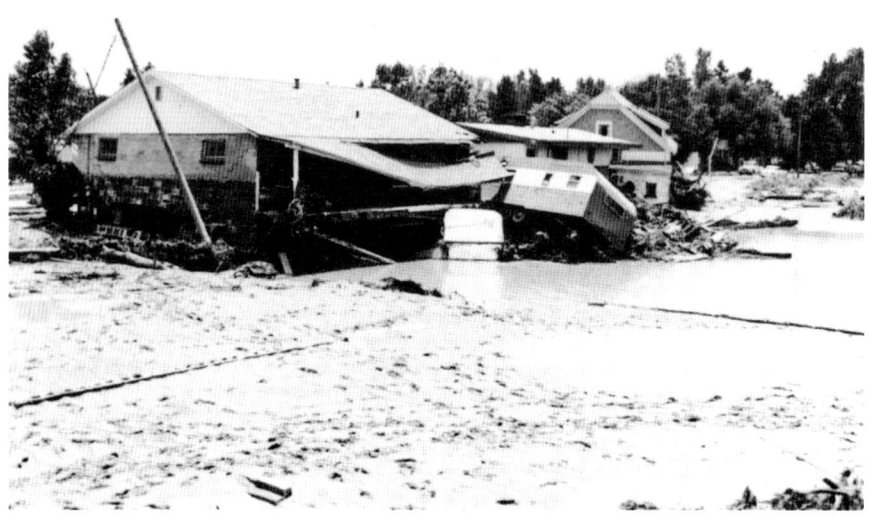

Houses damaged in the 1965 South Platte flood. *Courtesy of Colorado Department of Natural Resources.*

climbed into bed, their father opened their doors again to tell them it was time to evacuate.

The family heard the screeching sirens as they raced for their car and drove up the hill to join approximately five hundred people who were sitting in their cars and trucks watching the muddy water flood their town. When it was done, only seven homes remained untouched by the flood. Everhart states that when he finally returned home, "Our front yard was covered with about a foot of mud along with a dead pig and cow."

Three of the reservoirs west of Pikes Peak were destroyed in the flood, leaving a three-hundred-foot gorge above the town of Gillett.

## LITTLETON AND THE DEATH OF THE HORSES

On June 16, the heavy rains came. Larkspur had fourteen inches of rain, a massive cloudburst creating a churning, raging wall of water twenty feet high slamming down Plum Creek. A twenty-three-year-old man was killed in Larkspur, when he was surprised by the flooding and crashed his vehicle through a barricade. The water hit the South Platte River and Cherry Creek. It rolled into Littleton first, but the people of that town had at least an hour's warning. It wasn't enough. The flood took its first victims at the Columbine Country Club before spreading out toward the racetrack.

Centennial Racetrack opened for horse racing in 1950; ten thousand people walked through the gates on opening day, according to the City of Littleton website. According to Woody Senier, breeder/owner/trainer at Centennial, "It was not like a little hometown racetrack, it was big, and people would come from all over the country to race at Centennial."

The rain began to fall in Littleton on June 16, 1965. Charlie Vail, a partner with the Littleton Large Animal Clinic, described the storm in a City of Littleton video: "There was a downspout rain up on the east and west Plum Creek and a huge amount of water fell in a very short time and created in those drainage ditches, really, a tidal wave. The river didn't rise, the river just flushed right down, and it was unbelievably devastating."

Red Finch, a jockey working at Centennial at the time of the flood, is also quoted in the video. "I seen a wall of water come through there and, in fact, we were on the racetrack with horses and we left riding and went up to the higher hills and I spent four days in a two-car garage with a horse that I rode in a race because of the flood, we couldn't get back." Finch also recalls seeing five horses that panicked and climbed to the top floors of the grandstand, four stories high.

The owners of the racehorses were advised to move their horses as soon as possible, but many owners lived out of state, so the employees at the track moved the horses to the barn area. According to Woody Senier, that's where one hundred horses drowned. Ingrid Knotts, office manager of the Colorado Thoroughbred Breeders Association, states in the video that she believed there was a state of panic at Centennial and people didn't know what to do, "and I think that there were too many horses killed."

The roof of the shed rows collapsed, trapping many animals in the mud. It was days before they could be rescued or their bodies recovered. In the end, more horses died than were saved, but this was not due to lack of effort. It was the flood. It was the rain.

Local residents speculated that the death of the animals and the severe damage would be the end of the racetrack, but it actually opened only four days late for the racing season. Many residents credited Centennial's general manager, Ivan Thomas, for this accomplishment.

## THE SOUTH PLATTE WASTE DUMP

Closer to Denver, the South Platte had become a "waste dump" over the years, according to Pat Massengill writing on the City of Littleton website. The river around Denver "was littered with abandoned cars, refrigerators, construction debris and everything else that people looked to discard. In 1965, there was an accounting for that lack of respect for the South Platte River," Massengill explains. The *Colorado Springs Business Journal* referred to the situation as Denver's "laissez-faire policy toward dumping and pollution."

When the water wall hit the South Platte around Denver, it swept up all of this trash in the river and literally created a twenty-foot wall of refuse with vehicles of every kind, including mobile homes; massive trees ripped from the ground with their roots still intact; shrubs and landscaping; large and small chunks of houses; animals; and, sometimes, people screaming for help or already drowned.

Floodwater is not clear, creek water, it is a combination of chemicals of every imaginable kind that are washed out of garages, homes and businesses. When people and animals fall into floodwaters, the chances of survival are slim, mainly because there is so much debris. In the 1965 flood, the debris was more visible than the water, due to the waste from the South Platte.

The floodwall crashed violently into Denver, destroying twenty-six bridges; chopping roads into chunks of asphalt; and shattering homes, businesses and other structures, including two power plants. Moving north and northeast, the flood snatched water from Sand and Clear Creeks, and the Bijou, Little Beaver and Poudre Rivers. The floodwaters began to spread into Sterling, Fort Morgan and Brush, destroying homes, businesses, farms and, according to Massengill, "a quarter-million-acres of farmland."

## WHEN THE FLOOD WAS OVER

The floodwaters continued to flow through Colorado until June 20. It is estimated that between twenty-one and twenty-four people died in the floods of 1965, but in a statewide flood of that magnitude, it is nearly impossible to determine the loss of life. Financial losses are estimated at around $540 million ($4 billion updated). More than 1,700 buildings were destroyed in Denver alone, and more than 67 percent of the industrial portions of the city was completely destroyed.

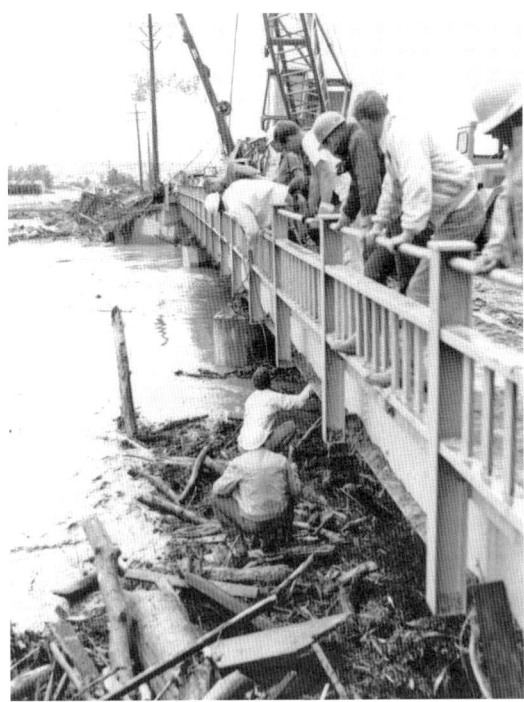

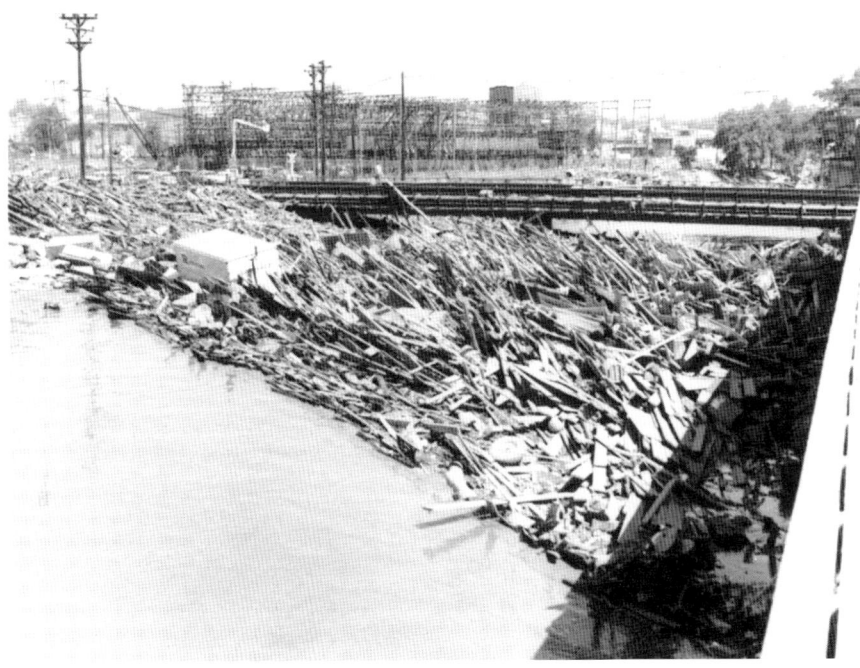

*This page*: Bridge damage and extensive debris flow from the 1965 South Platte River flood. *Courtesy of Colorado Department of Natural Resources.*

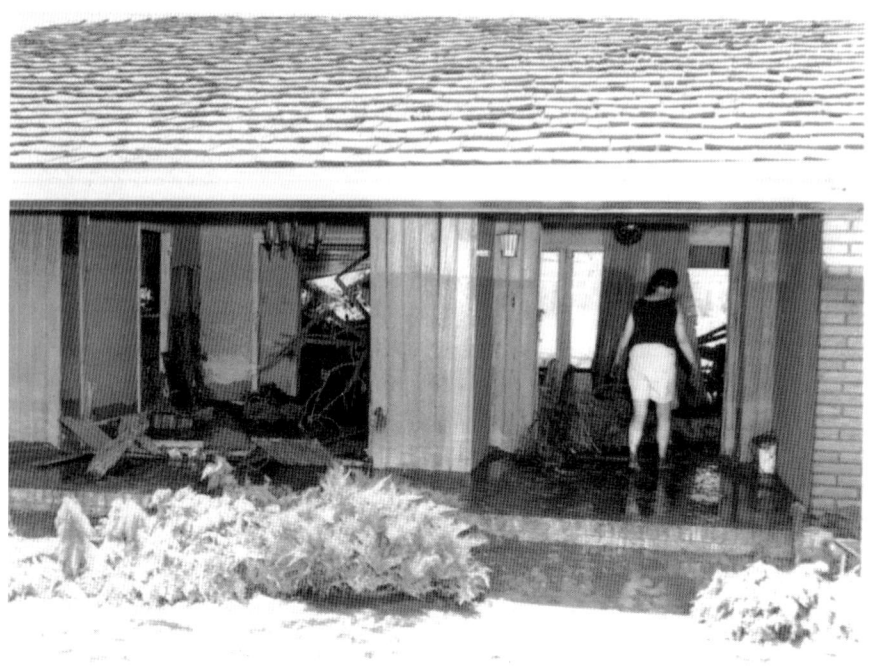

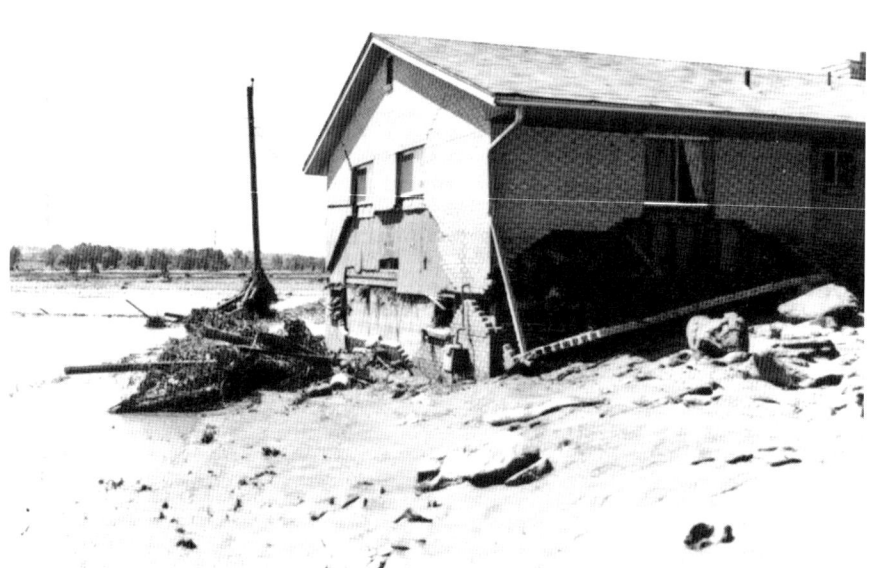

*This page*: Houses damaged in the South Platte River flood of 1965. *Courtesy of Colorado Department of Natural Resources.*

If there was a positive side to the floods of 1965, the City of Denver began construction on Chatfield Dam within months of the floods. The dam was completed in 1972, seven years later. The city also built a dam at Bear Creek.

The floods brought attention to the condition of the South Platte River and its use as a waste dump. Workers were hired to clean up the river, and efforts were made to maintain the river in a healthier condition.

# 9

# THE BIG THOMPSON CANYON FLOOD

## NATIONAL CELEBRATION TURNED TRAGEDY IN 1976

*I Am the River, I Hurt too!*
*Please don't be angry with me, I was just doing what God intended of me.*
*I am just a small stream. I could only hold so much, I really tried hard.*
*The rains from above multiplied as it came down.*
*The force became too great for me. I could no longer hold it within my banks.*
*You know the feeling, when too much gets put on you, and you sometimes fall apart.*
*Don't be angry with me, I hurt too. My rocks were tossed about and my trees ripped up.*
*My beauty was no more. I too have lost, for the very same people you loved and lost, also loved me.*
*They came in the summer to listen to my rippling sound,*
*to dip their feet in my cool waters at the end of a long day.*
*They sat and smelled the pine trees and watched the deer drink from my stream.*
*The ones who lived beside me year after year, I heard their laughter and I saw their tears.*
*I miss their sounds, their sitting along my banks after a day at work,*
*just to relax and say how lucky they were and how beautiful I was.*
*I liked that; we had great respect for each other.*
*Don't be angry with me. Years have passed.*
*I guess some of my beauty has returned, at least people say so.*
*I have some trees and bushes again, but deep down I will never be the same.*
*I loved those folks, too.*
*Just remember I was trying to do what was intended for me,*
*and maybe someday, you will no longer be angry with me.*
*—Barb Anderson, secretary of the Big Thompson Flood Memorial*

On May 23, 1976, American folk singer and songwriter Bob Dylan performed a concert at Hughes Stadium in Fort Collins, Colorado. The partly recorded concert is included in his album *Hard Rain*. Ironically, it did rain, a hard and steady rain that continued throughout the entire concert.

The city of Denver set a record. Between May 21 and 22, 1976, 6.53 inches of rain fell in twenty-four hours.

Were these omens? Signs of terrible things to come? Perhaps. A few short months later, in July 1976, between twelve and fourteen inches of rain fell on nearby Estes Park, spawning the most devastating and deadly flash flood in northern Colorado's history.

It was not supposed to be that way—so painful, so deadly. It was a time of celebration. July 1976 marked the 200th anniversary of the proclamation of independence from England made by America's thirteen original colonies. It was the 100th anniversary of Colorado's statehood, which is why Colorado is also called the "Centennial State."

It was also the height of the tourist season. The Big Thompson Canyon is popular for its good fishing, attractive campgrounds and rental cabins on the banks of the river. Hewlett-Packard had its company picnic at a park near Estes Park on that day. The hotels and campgrounds were full, and even part-time residents were at home in the Big Thompson Canyon that night, enjoying the holiday. It is estimated that between 2,500 and 4,000 people were in the canyon on July 31, 1976.

## THE STORM THAT BROUGHT THE FLOOD

The daily forecast, typical for Colorado summers in the 1970s, predicted "widely scattered showers." It wasn't raining in Loveland, at least not to any notable extent, and the black cloud that drew the attention of the people in Larimer County was actually hovering over Estes Park.

The explanation provided by NOAA states that a weak flow of moisture moving east began to strengthen on the east side of the Rocky Mountains near Larimer County. As the moist air was sliding up the mountain slopes, it mixed with the summertime heat to form one of the "scattered thunderstorms" predicted earlier in the day. Strong winds found along the mountain crests at ten thousand feet generally push these storms out of the area.

On the evening of July 31, 1976, the winds were weaker than normal, creating a stationary storm that grew in strength and intensity, lifting along

Colorado's Front Range, forming the black cloud that so many witnesses still remember, a thick cloud with intense density that fascinates meteorologists to this day. It is the cloud that people in Loveland recall seeing on that day, spread across Estes Park like a suffocating blanket.

The rain began to fall around 6:00 p.m. and continued for over three hours, dumping between twelve and fourteen inches on Estes Park, Drake and Glen Haven. Eight inches fell in one hour. But this Colorado cloudburst was different. Due to changes made to the river's path and the shape of the canyon, the water wall was a massive twenty feet high moving at fourteen miles per hour.

The floodwall crashed straight down the mountain like a giant construction truck loader, ripping century-old trees out by their roots, tossing boulders into the river like children's toys and reaching like a claw to snag every house, camper, trailer and tent. It swept up pickup trucks and cars filled with families trying desperately to escape.

Survivors remember the smell of dead animals, propane, chemicals of all kinds and raw sewage—the Estes Park sewage system was swept into the

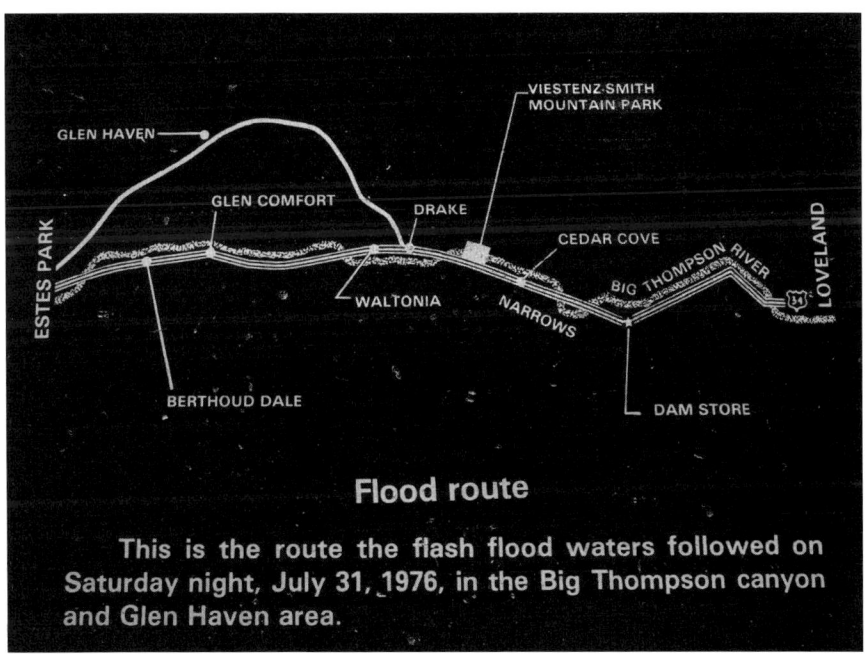

Plaque displaying the path of the Big Thompson Flood of 1976 displayed at the Viestenz-Smith Mountain Park near Highway 34. The park was built in 1925, destroyed by flooding in 1976 and rebuilt and destroyed again in 2013. *Photo taken in 2012 by Darla Sue Dollman.*

flood, as well. Telephone lines in Estes Park were down, and the people of Estes Park could do nothing to warn their neighbors of the disaster coming their way.

One of the most vivid memories of survivors scrambling up the sides of the mountains or clinging to tree branches was the sight of the giant water wall crashing down the canyon with strange, flashing lights coming from inside. As the waterwall passed, the horrified survivors realized the flashing lights were the headlights of vehicles filled with people screaming for help, but they were already beyond help. The floodwall exploded from the narrows, hit the highway and sent chunks of asphalt flying through the air.

## SACRIFICE

According to an interview with amateur radio communications officer Bill Green, published in *The Big Thompson Disaster*, it's possible that the first flood warning, as well as the first calls for help, came from another amateur radio operator who kept his equipment in his car. The man was near Drake and reported water on the road. There were also reports of rockslides. The dispatcher sent Colorado State Patrol sergeant Hugh Purdy to investigate. Purdy, who was off duty and watching television with his wife, left his home as soon as he received the call and headed for the canyon.

## THE LAST WORDS OF HUGH PURDY

The following words were spoken at approximately 9:00 p.m. on July 31, 1976, by Sergeant Willis Hugh Purdy of the Colorado State Patrol as he raced up Highway 34 from Loveland toward Drake, trying to find the source or location of the flood: "You better have Loveland starting to contact people along the Thompson east of the Narrows. I'm about two and a half…east of Drake and the river is pretty good, so it's going to be coming down better than this later. Call the power plant on the Thompson and advise them to get everybody out of the low in there."

Then, at 9:15 p.m.: "I'm right in the middle of it. I can't get out…about one-half mile east of Drake on the highway…to get out of the low area down below."

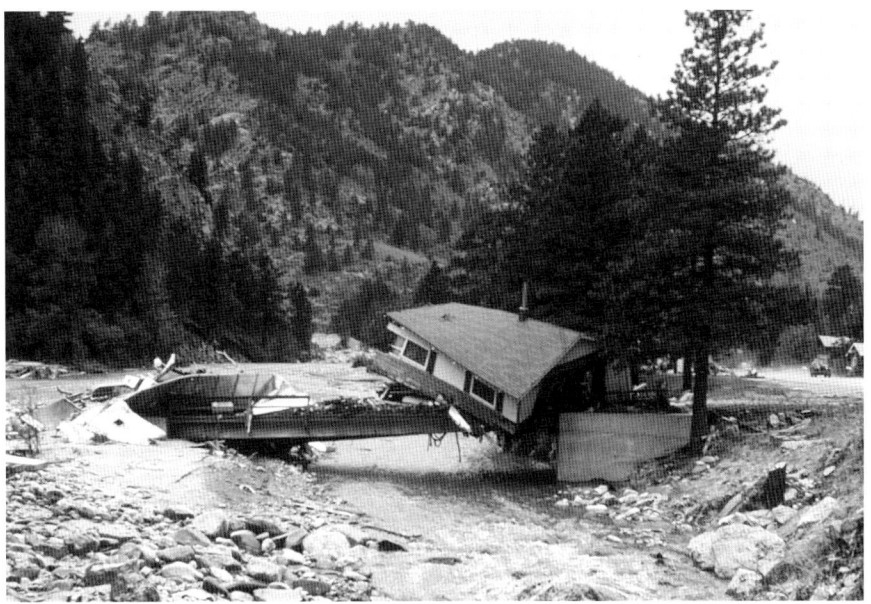

A cabin is lodged on a private bridge just below Drake during the Big Thompson Flood of July 31, 2013. Photo taken looking upstream. *Photo by W.R. Hansen, U.S. Geological Survey, August 13, 1976.*

The body of Sergeant Purdy was found approximately eight miles from the site of this last radio transmission. When his car was located, it was crushed beyond recognition. Purdy's vehicle was identified by a key ring with the inscription, "Colorado State Patrol." He sacrificed his life for the people in the Big Thompson Canyon. His last words were for the people.

## THE COLORADO STATE PATROL

Clark Champ's *Flood* states that the Colorado Highway Patrol office in Greeley received reports of a washout and rockslides on Highway 34 around 8:00 p.m. The call went out to Colorado state trooper William Miller, who was on patrol near Drake, according to the Colorado State Patrol. He was sent to Estes Park to investigate.

At 8:35 p.m., Miller called in to report his location—seven and a half miles into the canyon. As soon as he arrived, his car was hit by a thirty-foot wall of water that washed across the highway. Miller said:

# Colorado's Deadliest Floods

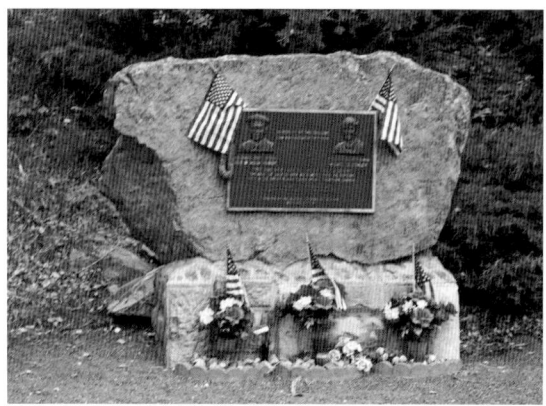

The Big Thompson Flood Memorial reads: "In Memory Of Sgt. W. Hugh Purdy / Michel O. Conley Colorado State Patrol / Estes Park Patrolman / They Gave Their Lives To Save The Lives Of Others The Night Of July 31, 1976 When More Than 140 Persons Died In The Great Flash Flood of Big Thompson Canyon." Dedicated on July 31, 1978. *Photo taken in 2012 by Darla Sue Dollman.*

"We've got to start taking people out! My car's gonna be washed away! I've got a real emergency down here!" Seconds later, his voice rose to a shout: "The whole mountainside is gone!" he said. "There is no way! I'm trying to get out of here before I drown!" Miller managed to swim to safety, but he didn't stop. He joined one of the sheriff's officers, traveling to campgrounds and homes to warn people about the flood. He later assisted in caring for the injured.

Colorado state trooper Timmie Littlejohn was also dispatched to Drake to prevent residents from driving into the canyon. He argued with one family, refusing to relent when they insisted on traveling past the barrier to reach the Waltonia Motel where they were staying. The Waltonia Motel was crushed in the flood. Another motel was completely destroyed in the flood; all of the registered occupants were killed. The register was later found near the Kansas border, the only remaining evidence that the motel ever existed.

Trooper Littlejohn was gradually surrounded by seventy-five people arguing with him that they should be allowed to drive down the mountain, but he refused. Littlejohn knew he was also trapped in the canyon, but he continued his rescue efforts.

Michael Owen Conley, an off-duty police officer and Vietnam veteran, was familiar with responding to emergencies. He was driving through the canyon with his wife, Phyllis, when they noticed the rise in the water. Conley also noticed a large boulder partially blocking the road.

Conley told his wife to leave the car and climb to safety, then he called the Colorado State Patrol and advised them to stop all vehicles from entering the canyon. Conley raced through the canyon trying to warn as many people as he could to climb to high ground. Phyllis spent a harrowing night on the mountainside with other survivors. According to the Officer Down Memorial

Page website, Michael Conley was personally responsible for saving at least sixty people before he drowned in the flood.

As soon as Sheriff Robert Watson heard of the flood, he worked feverishly to establish a command post at the base of the mountain and coordinate rescue efforts. The morning after the flood, Watson was told the rescue helicopters couldn't fly in the canyon due to rain. Instead, Watson organized volunteers in four-wheel-drive vehicles and horse patrols to search for and rescue survivors.

## A SURVIVOR'S PERSPECTIVE

Barb Anderson is the cofounder of the Big Thompson Canyon Flood Memorial. In 1970, Barb and her family moved to their home at 1901 Big Thompson Canyon Road, ten miles west of Loveland near the base of the towering cliffs. "When you arrived at The Dam Store the walls were straight up and down and the road curved for the three miles to our house," she explained. "It was to be our permanent home," she said, a place of safety and security for Barb, her husband, Andy, and their daughter Pam, who was twelve at the time, and Tina, who was nine.

Five years later, Anderson and her husband purchased the home of a neighbor, which was on the water's edge. It was their dream home, a home on the river. The Anderson family worked hard to remodel their new house and protected it with insurance, but at that time, few people realized that homeowner's insurance does not cover floods.

Anderson remembers when her mother-in-law came to visit on July 27. Her mother-in-law bought a Tiffany lampshade, and it was placed in the basement for temporary storage. Her mother-in-law suggested storing it upstairs in case of flood, and Anderson told her she'd take care of it later, then her mother-in-law returned home. "I assured her we didn't have floods here," Anderson said. "We never gave it a thought." Four days later, the canyon flooded. "We never thought it would happen again," she said. The canyon flooded again in 2013.

## SERGEANT PURDY'S WARNING

On July 31, 1976, Barb and Andy Anderson were in their living room watching the Olympics. Their children were in bed. They noticed a large, black cloud that seemed to cover Estes Park but didn't give it much thought.

At 8:45 p.m., they saw Sergeant Hugh Purdy's vehicle through their picture window. He had a bullhorn and shouted at the Andersons to get out of their house, then raced back up the canyon.

"About 15 minutes later, a friend who lived seven miles up the canyon called to ask how the river was, she said they were having heavy rain." Barb checked out the back door with a flashlight, but couldn't see anything of concern. Her friend told her to watch the water levels. Andy became concerned and decided to check on their neighbors.

Five minutes later, Barb's friend called again and told her to wake up her children and the neighbors and get to high ground. "The Waltona Motel is gone, the SS Rapids [motel] is gone!"

Barb called her neighbors to the east and told them it was time to get out, but they were setting up their river pump and packing their car, gathering their valuables. "Let it go and meet us up on the highway!" Barb warned. She called her neighbors and told them to send Andy home and that she would return for them. She needed Andy to get her own family. She couldn't get her dog to come out of the garage. Barb never saw her dog again.

She called as many people as she could on their four-party line, then the electricity and phone went out. That's when she knew the flood had hit the power plant, which was only half a mile west of their home.

"We were trying to get our neighbors, Fern and Grandma Kunce, her mother, into our car, but no one was in a hurry. We were still sitting in our car with a raging river twenty feet away." Anderson's husband appeared to be growing concerned. "He wanted to pick up Grandma Kunce and carry her as she walked with a walker, but she said she didn't want to hurt him."

Barb Anderson could hear that the river was growing more violent. She grabbed a flashlight and ran to the corner of the house to check the river. "I was glad I did not scream or tell anyone to come look, because the water was going so fast." Anderson watched piles of debris float past. She could see boards, indicating that houses or other structures were breaking apart.

When everyone was in the car, Andy Anderson turned the vehicle to the east, because the water was coming from the west. They were driving up the hill when they noticed that the son of a neighbor, who was around twelve, had opened the gate for them. They told him to join them in their station

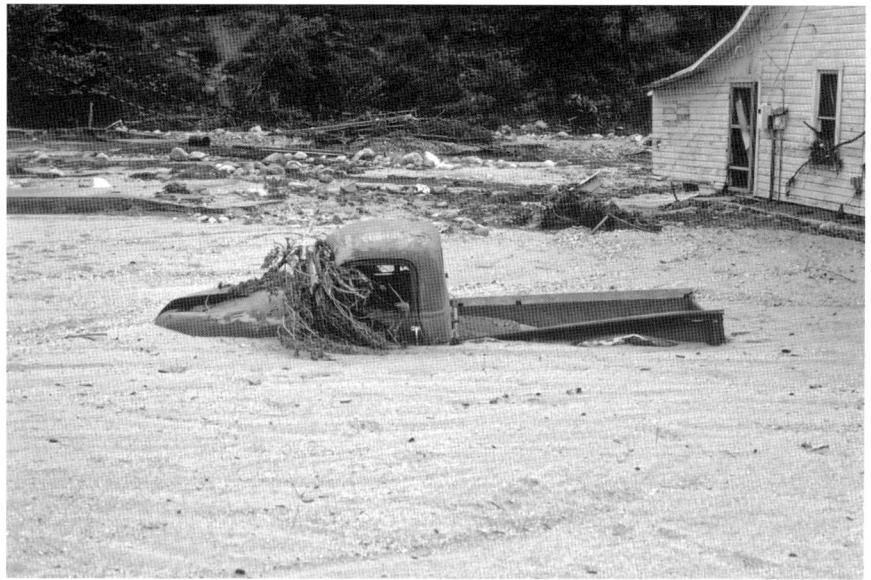

A pickup truck is partly buried in a sand blanket deposited by the North Fork Big Thompson River at Drake during the Big Thompson Flood. Note flood debris in the windows of the house on the right. *Photo by W.R. Hansen, August 13, 1976. U.S. Geological Survey.*

wagon. When the boy climbed into the car, he told the group that the water was right behind them. "I thought about it afterwards. That kid was right there, too. He could have been gone in a heartbeat," Barb recalls. She later learned that the boy's older brother, Rick Huffsmith, nineteen, had died in the flood. He had left earlier to drive up the canyon to meet friends. The boy was probably waiting for his brother at the gate.

The Andersons and neighbors reached Highway 34; it was there that they spent the night. They watched as cars floated past in the river, lights flashing. They heard and smelled the hiss of propane tanks spilling their contents into the water and watched as the tanks acted like battering rams against trees and houses.

## THE REALITY OF FLOOD RECOVERY

The reality of recovery from a catastrophic flood is that no one ever completely recovers, especially from their memories. The following morning was even more painful for the Andersons; they learned that Rick Huffsmith had died in the flood, along with their neighbor's grandson and great-grandson. Also killed were their neighbors in Cedar Cove, the Graham family, including Clara (sixty-four), Beverly (thirty-three), Teresa (ten)—her body was never found—and Lisa (two). "Bob Graham and his son, the father of the two children, were both spared to endure the heartache. I babysat the children. You never get over it," she said. "We lost Doc Lee, Claude and Mae Schell, Keith Baily, Ken and Nora Huffnagle and the rest of the 144, including those who were never found. Many families lost their pets and all of their belongings."

"On Saturday morning, a helicopter started taking people out of the canyon. We waited until last." The Andersons had a parakeet that survived, so she put him in the strainer of a kettle and covered it with a tea towel, and he chirped the entire day. When they boarded the helicopter, one of the rescuers asked what was in the teakettle and laughed when they told him it was their pet bird.

The Andersons were evacuated to a large field in west Loveland, then they were taken to Van Buren Elementary in Loveland. There they found neighbors and friends, but also discovered how many people had died that night. "We saw our neighbors, Bob and LeRoy Graham, so sad and lost. We hugged and cried. What can you say? As we walked away, I passed out." Anderson was taken to a doctor and given a sedative. She slept the rest of the day. "Even after that, we still had to face it all," she said.

The Andersons spent a few nights with an eighty-year-old friend in her one-bedroom apartment. Barb was concerned about how the trauma was affecting her two daughters. She moved her family to the home of another friend who had a child the same age as Barb's daughter Pam. Barb was still in shock from the flood, asking herself, "How could this be happening?"

The Andersons didn't have time to gather anything they might need. They had no clothing with them, no possessions to help calm their daughters. "I felt like I was in a dream and had not awakened yet, but I was still walking around." Barb remembers all the people who were trying to help, the donations, the woman with a basket of embroidered tea towels who made certain everyone received one of her gifts. "That was very special," she said.

The Andersons moved away from the river, back into their house farther up the mountain, which was spared in both the 1976 and 2013 floods. Barb was asked why she stayed in the canyon. She explained:

*Everyone lives in a place they love, and if it be in Iowa, or Kansas, and they have a tornado and their house is destroyed they will likely build back, first because it is their land, and second because they love the place. There is no guarantee that a disaster will or will not happen again.*

*So it is with the river, no doubt about it. People love the river. If they choose to live near it that should be their choice, not the decision of the government or anyone else. Know the dangers of the area and don't try to second-guess the danger of a flood. Always have a plan. Get to the highest place around and don't go back for anything. Watch the weather. Be prepared.*

## THE RESCUE EFFORT

According to *The Big Thompson Disaster*, the Larimer County Sheriff's Office in Estes Park sent out a call for help before the flood crested. Within fifteen minutes, fifty-five National Park Service personnel responded and were on their way to the river with heavy equipment, attempting to mitigate the flood damage before it even started down the mountain.

More than one hundred members of local law enforcement arrived the following morning to help with the rescue and recovery. The National Guard was called out to assist. Volunteers from surrounding towns crowded the highways leading into Loveland. On August 2, 1976, Larimer County was declared a disaster area by President Gerald Ford.

It was reported that between eleven and fourteen helicopters flew through the canyon searching for survivors and victims. One of the survivors rescued from the flood said he saw a young girl clinging to a branch in a tree. Rescuers were unsure of the risk of flying in the rain, but they searched for her anyway. She was rescued by helicopter and reunited with her family, who were waiting at Loveland High School. At least fifty people were airlifted from a field near what was once Glen Haven. That town was almost completely destroyed by the flood.

It was nearly impossible for family members to obtain information about missing relatives, even those who lived nearby. Fort Collins resident Fred Bogard recalls the fear he felt for his family when he learned of the flood. His sister and her family lived forty-five miles outside the Big Thompson Canyon. "We were unable to reach them after the flood, so my father and I attempted to drive down….We were unable to get there due to road closures and a small bridge washed out between Loveland and Fort Collins. We did finally hear from them that day—they were all safe! The water in the river during the flood crossed an open field on the opposite side of the river from their property. Water came up as close as twelve feet from their house, but they [had] no damage to the main house."

Fort Collins resident David R. Grant also remembers the flood. "I was eleven years old at the time," he said. "My most vivid memory was listening to the list of hundreds of names being read over the radio stations of people that were unaccounted for, seeking information from anyone who knew their whereabouts."

Cindi Hendrix's grandfather Lowell Watts was the extension director at Colorado State University. Her family was in the flood and was one of the first families extracted from the canyon by helicopter. It is their story that most people remember from watching the news reports.

The family was trapped in their cabin when the floodwaters hit, and Cindi Hendrix's little brother, three-year-old Aaron Watts, died in the flood. His mother, Deborah Watts, wrote a book about their experience called *A Flood of Memories* to try to help with the pain and loss. After the flood, Cindi's grandfather helped search for survivors. "There were so many heroes throughout this disaster," Cindi said. "We had many heroes in our nightmare/rescue."

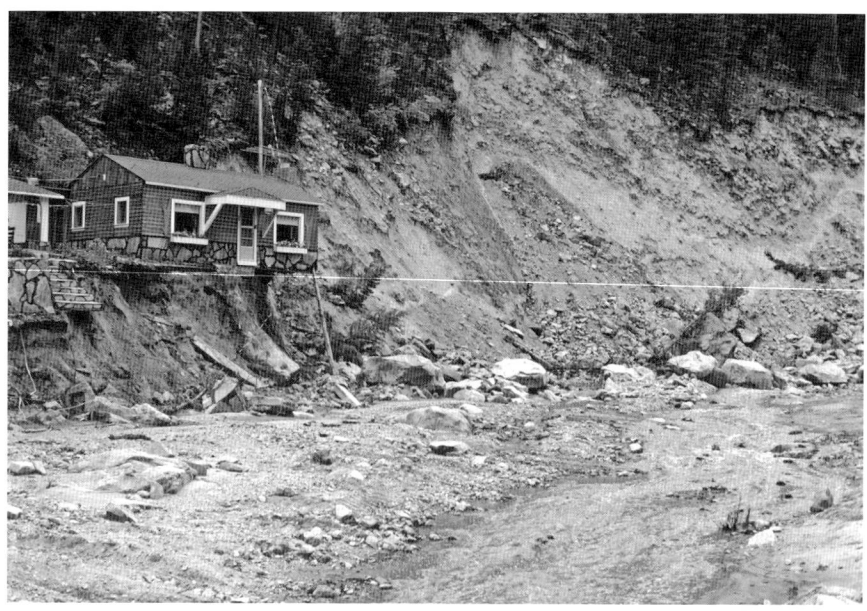

A house precariously balanced near the floodwaters below Glen Comfort during the Big Thompson Flood of 1976. *Photo by R.R. Shroba, August 13, 1976, U.S. Geological Survey.*

## WHEN MEMORIES BECOME NIGHTMARES

Mary Myers was fifteen years old when she witnessed the flood in the canyon. "Somehow, the '76 flood stole our innocence in a sweet lazy canyon with summer residents and visitors," Myers explained.

"From our location below Drake, we could not see the extent of the cloud that covered the canyon," she said. "It never rained heavily where we were. There was a lot of lightning, and it was not untypical that the power was out."

Myers and her family became concerned around 9:00 p.m. "I saw cars stop and people taking flashlights up the mountain across from us. I went to the driveway to see what was going on. It was there I heard the roar of the wall of water coming down the canyon. It was lit from the inside by the cars it swallowed whole. The swollen river was moving too fast to leave its banks, and I remember I was actually looking up at the crest of the water in the deepest part of the channel before I ran back up to the cabin."

"An hour into the flood, I saw a car up against our bridge," she continued. "In the flashing strobe of lightning I saw a driver trying to get out using the bridge rail. Then the crack as the bridge gave way at that moment washing one of the flood's victims to their demise."

"Propane tanks hissed down the river and left a smell that filled the canyon. At 4:00 a.m., we thought somehow that rescue was already in the canyon when we saw spotlights illuminating the mountainside…only to find out it was cars with their lights on, bobbing down the river."

"The next afternoon, we were evacuated. My grandmother went in the first Chinook helicopter. I was tasked with helping our visiting elderly neighbors and their pets. They had a couple of dogs and I can't remember if it was three or five cats stuffed in a cardboard box. I will never forget the chaos inside the helicopter when the cats got out!"

## THOSE WHO WERE LOST

*Time* magazine lists the Big Thompson Canyon Flood of 1976 in the Top Ten Historic U.S. Floods. For many Colorado residents, the night of July 31, 1976, is one of their most terrifying memories. As we listened to the radio reports, read the stories in the newspapers and watched the heart-wrenching scenes on television, Coloradoans cried for the victims. We will

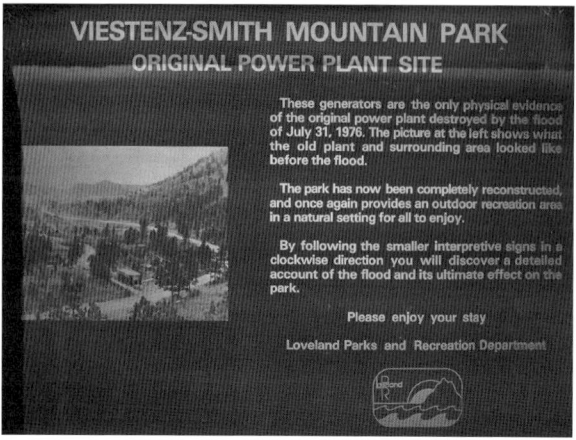

Plaque at Viestenz-Smith Mountain Park near Highway 34 in Big Thompson Canyon showing Loveland Light and Power plant, which opened in 1925 and describing the history of the park. The park was destroyed in the Big Thompson Canyon Flood of 1976, rebuilt, then destroyed again in the Colorado Floods of 2013. *Photo by Darla Sue Dollman.*

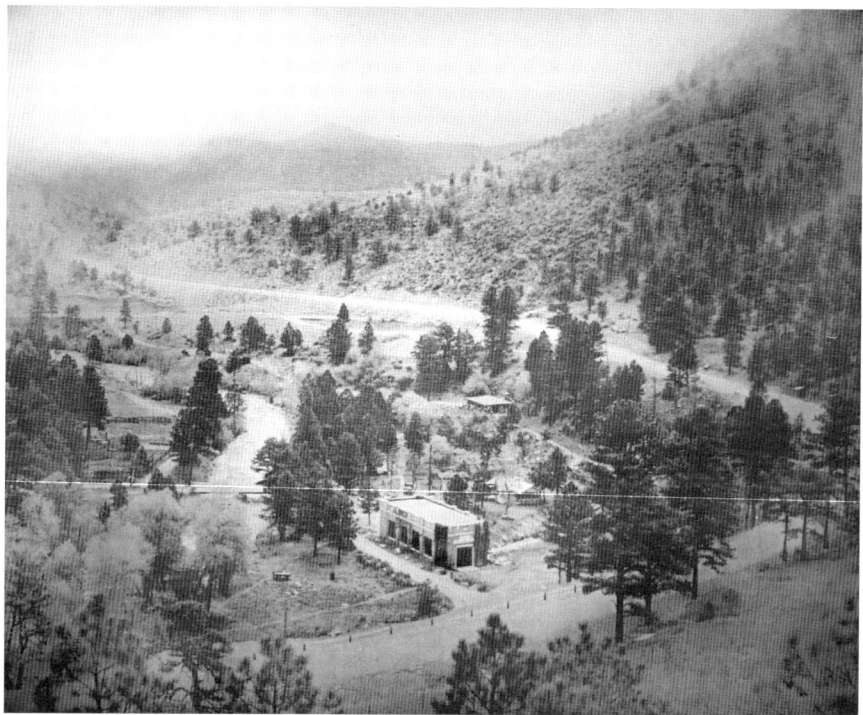

Photo on plaque at Viestenz-Smith Mountain Park near Highway 34 in Big Thompson Canyon showing the Loveland Light and Power plant, which opened in 1925. The park was destroyed in the Big Thompson Canyon Flood of 1976, rebuilt, then destroyed again in the Colorado Floods of 2013. *Photo by Darla Sue Dollman.*

all carry emotional scars for life, and they will return every time we drive through the canyon, knowing that somewhere beneath the roots of trees, boulders and spring flowers lie the bodies of victims who were never found: Teresa Graham (ten) of Cedar Cove; Evelyn Kindred (sixty-seven) from the town of Drake; George McCarty (twenty-one), a camper visiting from Denver; Vernon Oler (fifty-one) of Longmont; and Rochelle Rogers (two) of Brighton. They are a part of the canyon now.

Local funeral homes quickly realized that they were unable to handle the shocking number of victims, so the previously closed Loveland Memorial Hospital was reopened to serve as a temporary morgue.

It is believed that 144 people died in the Big Thompson Canyon flood and 150 people were injured. A study conducted by the USGS states that "the ages of the victims ranged from two years to 94 years, with about 40 percent of them under 30 years of age and 28 percent over 60 years old. About two-thirds of the victims were residents of Colorado; the other one-third were from 17 other States and the Philippine Islands."

According to NOAA, the flood destroyed 418 houses and floodwater damaged an additional 138. As for businesses, 152 were destroyed, some with little more than documents and memories left behind to indicate that they ever existed. Sources vary in terms of estimates, but it is believed that the Big Thompson Canyon Flood caused between $35 and $40 million in damages and loss.

## ALIVE AND WELL IN OKLAHOMA THIRTY-TWO YEARS LATER

Barb Anderson was also involved in what is perhaps one of the strangest stories to come out of the Big Thompson Flood disaster. Anderson and other survivors compiled information on the flood victims and survivors in an effort to make sure everyone was accounted for in the aftermath. Anderson was also working on information for a bronze memorial. She kept coming back to Darrell Johnson. His "missing" status bothered Anderson, and she finally made the difficult decision to keep his name off the bronze memorial.

Johnson, listed among the missing, had rented a cabin at the Sleepy Hollow Resort. All of the cabins were rented that night, and Johnson was given a room, but the cabins were safely evacuated before they were destroyed by the flood. Anderson couldn't figure out why they had a file for Johnson at the coroner's office but no information on him. He was listed as missing, or never recovered.

Anderson also knew that the previous owners of the Sleepy Hollow Resort were remodeling the cabins at the time of the flood, so she searched for the owner, who she was told was Billy North, a schoolteacher. She was unable to locate North.

While Anderson was preparing a breakfast for the Big Thompson Canyon Association, a woman volunteered to help. She introduced herself as Billie North, "and I about lost it!" Anderson said. "I thought Billy was a guy! So we laughed, and then we cried." Then she asked North to meet with her to discuss the mystery of Darrell Johnson. North confirmed that Johnson had checked into the hotel that night but said he wasn't alone—he had a wife and two young children with him.

Anderson knew she had to locate Johnson or add his name to the memorial. She returned to her search. She guessed that Johnson was in his twenties or thirties if he had two young children, which would make him around sixty when she resumed her search. She focused on all Darrell Johnsons in Oklahoma City in their sixties, taking a chance that he was still in the same city. Then she started making phone calls. It was her third call.

"I told him who I was and what I was doing. There was a pause, then he shouted to his wife and asked what year they were in Colorado." Johnson's wife confirmed that it was 1976.

Darrell Johnson, his wife and two children were still living in Oklahoma City. They had checked into the cabin in the canyon, then decided they wanted to travel to Denver instead and visit an amusement park. They ate at Casa Bonita and stayed at a different motel. They never told anyone at the Sleepy Hollow that they were leaving the canyon.

Johnson's relatives back in Oklahoma City knew he had intended to stay in the canyon that night and reported him as missing. Johnson never called the Sleepy Hollow to tell them he wasn't returning and never requested a refund. His family forgot to call and tell the investigators that he had arrived home safely. Darrell and his family drove home the next day and learned of the flood on the news.

Anderson sent Johnson a copy of *The Big Thompson Disaster* to show that he was listed as missing. A year later, Johnson returned to Colorado to visit Anderson. He told her he wanted to come back for the next memorial, but he died of cancer a short time later. Strangely, Anderson said, the man who was missing all those years and believed to be dead owned and ran two funeral homes in Oklahoma.

## REASONS FOR THE EXTREME DEVASTATION

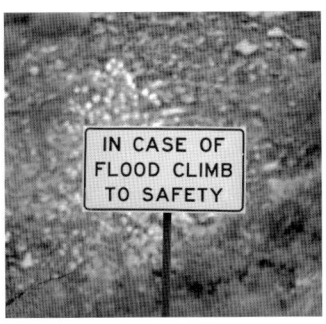

Water safety signs installed after the Big Thompson Flood of 1976 encouraging people to leave their vehicles and climb to higher ground in the case of floods. *Photo by Darla Sue Dollman, 2016.*

Several factors contributed to the devastation of the Big Thompson Canyon Flood: the record-breaking rainfall; the steep, narrow canyons; the rocky slopes; and the presence of thousands of people celebrating in the canyon on July 31, 1976. But there were a few additional reasons why the flood was so horrific: communication problems within the canyon; the lack of emergency instructions or warning signs for residents and visitors; the original construction of the highway; and communication issues with meteorologists.

First, there were no signs in the canyon instructing people to climb to higher ground, so they instinctively ran to their cars to escape the flood. A study conducted by FEMA showed that two out of three flash-flood deaths occur when people try to escape in their vehicles. Six inches of water is enough to touch the bottom of cars and enough to cause the driver to lose control of the vehicle—the flood is actually driving the car, not the driver. A foot of water will float most vehicles, and two feet drags them into the water. That includes SUVs and pickup trucks.

This is what happened in the Big Thompson Canyon Flood. According to a report compiled by the USGS and NOAA, more than 430 vehicles were found in the floodwater. Some of the vehicles caught in the floodwater were carried into the city of Loveland. There are now signs throughout the canyon warning drivers to leave their vehicles and climb to higher ground.

## ROAD CONSTRUCTION

*Colorado Experience* dedicated an episode to the Big Thompson Flood of 1976, including a brief history of the canyon. William Riley built the first road in 1903 to allow for easier access to Estes Park. The National Industrial Recovery Act, part of the New Deal, created funding for road projects, and one of these projects was a highway through the canyon, Highway 34, built

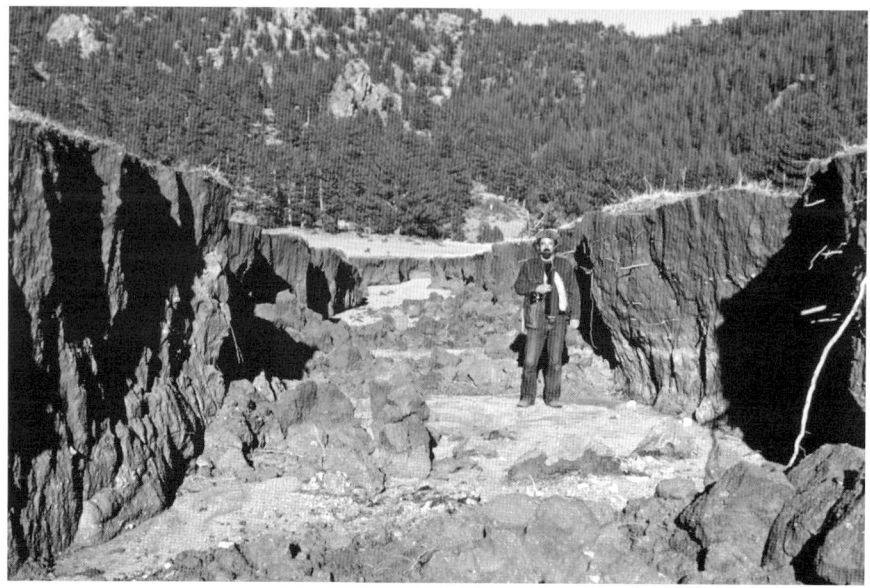

Dirt road washed out by drainage channeled into the roadway near Glen Haven during the Big Thompson Flood of July 31, 1976. *Photo by R.R. Shroba, September 20, 1976. U.S. Geological Survey.*

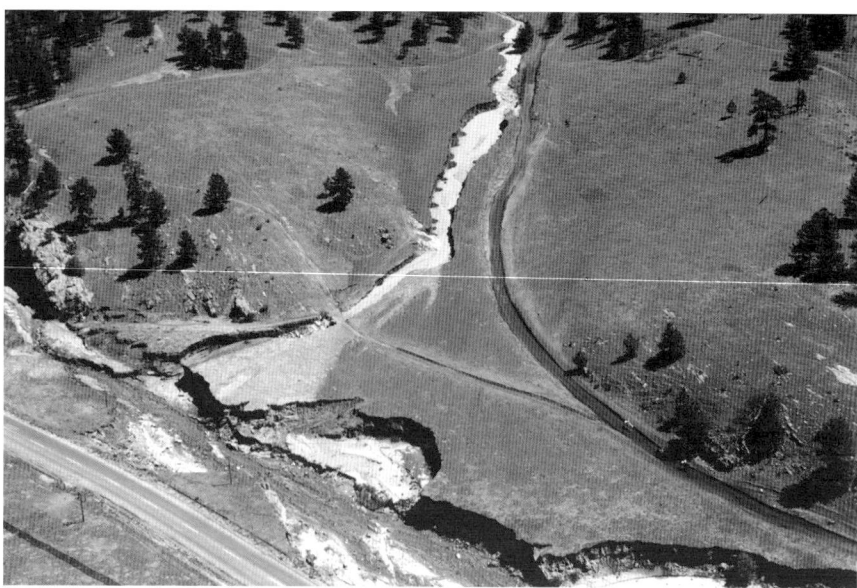

Big Thompson Canyon Flood. Deeply scoured alluvium along Dry Gulch and a tributary fan. Dry Gulch crested here at about 4,460 cubic feet per second. Note the evidence of overbank flow on the alluvial fan. *Photo by W.R. Hansen, August 13, 1976. U.S. Geological Survey.*

in 1926. In typical human fashion, when the highway was built, the engineers decided that nature didn't do a good enough job, so they realigned the river in twenty-seven places so that it could run alongside the highway. After the flood, a section of Highway 34 in "the Narrows" was raised sixteen feet.

With a river that ran in a straight line from the top to the bottom of the canyon, floods formed easily and often. The Big Thompson Canyon flooded twelve times before 1976 according to the USGS, but tourism and traffic in the canyon actually quadrupled between 1960 and 1970. The U.S. Army Corps of Engineers conducted a study of the Big Thompson Canyon in 1971 and predicted that "a serious flood could happen every six years." This was the first official statement to recommend flood insurance, but most people still do not realize that their home insurance does not cover floods.

After a second catastrophic flood in 2013, the Colorado Department of Transportation closed portions of Highway 34 in the Big Thompson Canyon to begin a massive reconstruction of the highway to raise the roadway, providing greater safety to travelers in times of flood, as well as increasing the capacity of the Big Thompson River Channel.

## COMMUNICATION DISASTER

One of the most painful realizations to come out of the Big Thompson Canyon Flood response was the fact that meteorologists knew there was flooding and did not even announce the possibility of such an event until the flood wall had already reached Loveland.

Doppler radar was invented in 1980, four years after the Big Thompson Canyon Flood. The flood notification system in 1976 was located in Limon in eastern Colorado. It was an unreliable system. According to *Colorado Experience: Big Thompson Flood*, the Limon system was constantly breaking down.

In addition, meteorologists reported that they were under pressure to refrain from reporting possible natural disasters too soon during tourist seasons. The television stations were also reluctant to interrupt coverage of the 1976 Olympic Games for a warning, but the flood was already underway by the time they received notification—news of the flood from Limon was generally delivered by fax, and the fax machine was broken. One news station finally ran a ticker at the bottom of the screen warning of possible flooding in the canyon, but many people in the canyon didn't have televisions because they were camping or staying in cabins.

## THE SIPHON

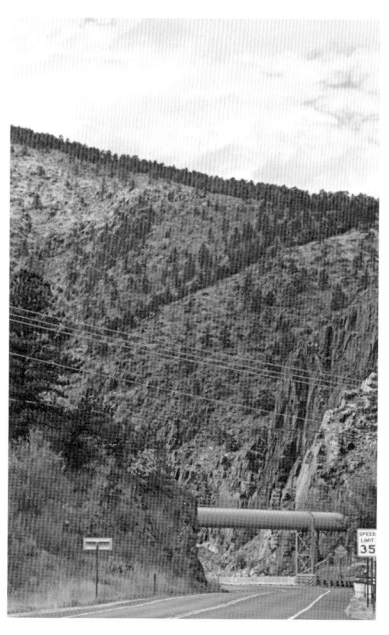

There is a thirty-five-ton metal cylinder reaching from across the canyon wall that is part of a complex water transportation system in the Colorado Rocky Mountains. This siphon was ripped from the mountainsides and collapsed into the debris flow during the Big Thompson Canyon Flood. The Eagle Construction Company replaced the siphon with a 220-foot long steel pipe at a cost of $187,000. The new pipe is green to blend in with its surroundings.

While the siphon was under repair, the water levels at Horsetooth Reservoir fell, and many residents, including Fred Bogard, were able to see a few remnants of the town of Stout.

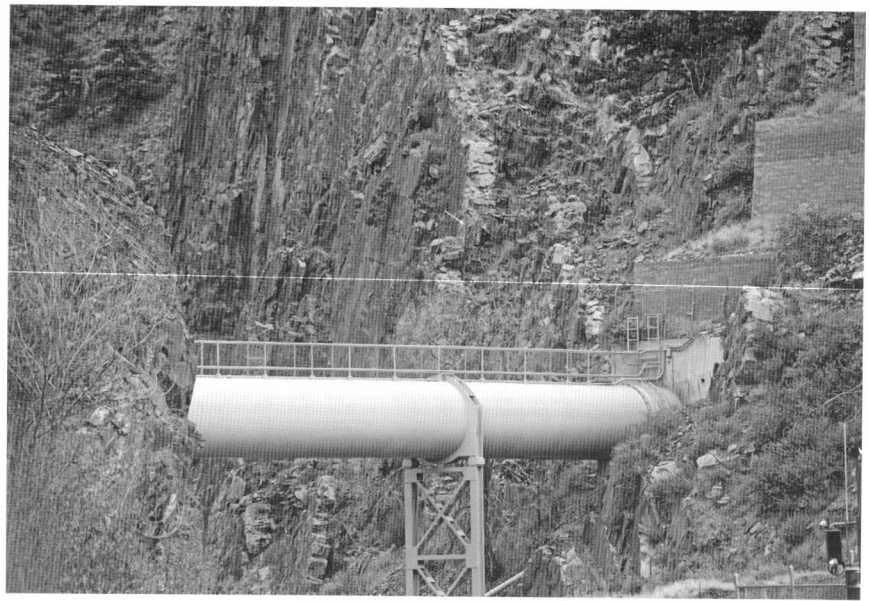

*This page*: The Big Thompson Canyon's Siphon. *Photo by Darla Sue Dollman, 2012.*

# 10
# THE LAWN LAKE DAM DISASTER OF 1982 IN ESTES PARK AND COLORADO'S DAMS

*You can't argue with a river, it is going to flow. You can dam it up, put it to useful purposes, deflect it, but you can't argue with it.*
—Dean Gooderham Acheson

Lawn Lake was created by one of the last glaciers to recede from what is now Rocky Mountain National Park. The twenty-six-foot-high earthen Lawn Lake Dam was built in 1902 with the intention of releasing water to help irrigate crops in Loveland during the summer months. Due to its remote location and the fact that it was nearly impossible to maintain, dam inspections ended and the road that led to the dam was eventually swallowed up by the surrounding forest.

According to a report by the National Park Service Geologic Resources Division, the Colorado state engineer determined the dam failure was caused by "deterioration of lead caulking on the joint between the outlet pipe and the gate valve leading to the earth fill dam." In layman's terms, the dam failed because no one cared, and eventually, it was forgotten.

It was 6:00 a.m. on July 19, 1982, when the eighty-year-old Lawn Lake Dam collapsed, sending 3,000,000 gallons of water at eighteen thousand cubic feet per second in a thirty-foot waterwall racing toward the popular mountain town of Estes Park. Four campers disappeared in the floodwater that poured down Roaring River Valley, joined Fall River at Horseshoe Park and smashed into Cascade Dam, which was located seven miles from Lawn Lake. When it crushed Cascade Dam, 3,912,000 more gallons of

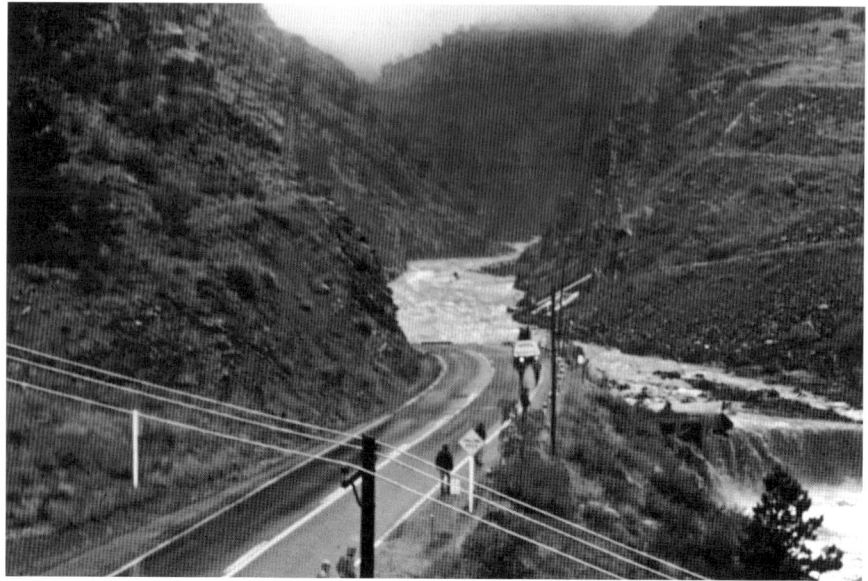

Floodwaters from the Lawn Lake Dam Disaster of 1982 joined with the Big Thompson River, which previously flooded in 1976. This photo shows sections of Highway 34 destroyed by the Big Thompson Flood on July 31, 1976. *U.S. Geological Survey.*

water joined the flood. The floodwaters then flowed into the Big Thompson River not far from the original source of the Big Thompson Canyon Flood of 1976.

By the time the wall of water and debris hit Elkhorn Avenue, the main street of the town of Estes Park, it was seven feet high; more than half of the flood that swept through the town was mud and debris collected by the water as it roared down the mountain.

The entire city of Estes Park and many of its residents might have disappeared forever, but a quick-thinking hero, Stephen Gillette, who was emptying trash cans in Rocky Mountain National Park that day, recognized the signs and sounds of the flood and ran to a mysterious phone to warn as many residents as possible.

The water slammed into Olympus Dam three hours and forty minutes after the flood started, then it stopped, filling the town of Estes Park with water, debris and over three feet of mud. The alluvial fan from the 1982 flood can still be seen on Fall River Road.

## THE EARLY DAYS

The area around Estes Park, Colorado, was a favorite of the Arapaho for many years. According to the *Estes Park Trail* newspaper, the Arapaho enjoyed visiting and camping in the area long before the Europeans arrived to participate in the same activities. In 1863, Joel Estes brought his family to the valley and invited *Rocky Mountain News* founder and editor William Byers. Byers wrote about the "pristine wilderness" and great beauty of the area. A town eventually formed, and it was named Estes Park. The town was also a favorite of writer, naturalist and explorer Isabella Bird.

The Fourth Earl of Dunraven arrived in the late 1800s and tried to take over Estes Park in a land grab that ended with Dunraven owning over six hundred acres. In 1903, construction began on a road that led from Loveland to Estes Park for the convenience of tourists and residents. In 1909, the famous Stanley Hotel was built by Freelan Oscar Stanley, creator of the Stanley Steamer, who moved to Colorado seeking a cure for tuberculosis in the clean mountain air.

The Stanley was built high on a mountainside overlooking the town and was a favorite of both tourists and residents, even more so when author Stephen King revealed that the Stanley was the inspiration for his novel *The Shining*. Stanley bought the land from Dunraven and intended to name it after the Earl of Dunraven. But the townspeople were so tired of Dunraven's shenanigans (he attempted to acquire all of the land in the surrounding area and make it a private hunting preserve) that they signed a petition insisting Stanley use his own name for the hotel.

The Stanley Hotel had an elevator, electric and gas lights, running water, telephones in every guest room and transportation to the nearby train depot. The hotel was state of the art when it was completed in 1909, and it increased tourism tremendously. It also inspired the establishment of Rocky Mountain National Park. With its increased popularity and population, Estes Park, located at the entrance to Rocky Mountain National Park, was incorporated in 1917 and remains one of the most popular tourist towns in Colorado.

In the summertime, Estes Park has an average population of forty thousand. On July 19, 1982, the residents and tourists of Estes Park were awakened around 6:00 a.m. They heard sounds described as a train, or a plane flying so low it could crash into the mountain. Instead, they discovered floodwaters crashing into the town, the last thing they were expecting to see on that sunny, summer morning.

## THE MYSTERY OF THE PHONE

At the time of the flood, Stephen Gillette's family owned the trash service that emptied the trash and recycling cans throughout the city of Estes Park and Rocky Mountain National Park. On July 19, 1982, there were a few trucks out for service, so Gillette was collecting the roadside cans.

"I was making my way toward Endo Valley when I first became aware that something was happening," Gillette explained. He heard a sound. He turned his head. What he saw next made his heart pound. "I saw a Ponderosa Pine in mid-air doing a loop the loop!" Gillette said.

"My first awareness that it might be the dam was when I heard the next set of sounds, like a plane crashing. I had no reason to believe a dam had actually broken, but that was my first thought due to the sounds I heard. I raced back to a pull-off area I noticed earlier. It had an emergency phone. I was told the phone didn't work. It was made clear to me that it was a "non-working phone." But that morning, it worked. I believe God made it work. That it was supposed to work that day."

It was Gillette's phone call that set off the chain of events leading to the safe rescue of the residents and most of the tourists in and around Estes Park.

"I called the park service headquarters and told them I saw something spectacular coming out of the water from Lawn Lake—trees flying through the air—and a park ranger arrived within minutes. I was standing on one side of the road and a park ranger was on the opposite side still setting up barricades when we watched the river take what was left of the bridge out of the area."

Gillette remained in the area as long as he could to help the park service. "I then drove up to Rainbow Curve so I could get a better view because it is much higher in elevation. It looked like a waterfall had formed coming out of the lake. In fact, I remember seeing a tourist nearby and she asked me for the name of that waterfall. I told her, 'Well, it only runs today.'"

Gillette quickly became a local hero. "All I did was make the phone call, though," he modestly explained. "The emergency workers did the important work."

Gillette drove his truck into the city to help with the clean-up work, along with the rest of the employees of the company. "We all helped," he said. "The people of the city all came together and pitched in. It was the beginning of a renewal for Estes Park, a dressing-up of the downtown area."

A few weeks later, the city of Estes Park, which was almost wiped out in one night, was once again in business. It held its annual Rooftop Rodeo, and Gillette was invited to participate in the parade. He was later invited to view the lake in a helicopter with the Bureau of Land Management. "It really didn't look that big," he said, "but it held back a lot of water. After the flood, though, many of the dams were removed from that area and in Rocky Mountain National Park because they were in such a state of disrepair that they were falling apart."

## WHEN THE FLOOD HIT ESTES PARK

The force of the floodwater in Estes Park was so strong that it flattened street signs, shattered windows and floated trucks and cars. But most of the damage was caused by three feet of mud left after the water moved on. There was so much mud that snowplows and bulldozers were needed to clean up the streets and parks and to haul the flood debris to the county dump, which is where Gillette and his coworkers were able to help. But homeowners and business owners still had three feet of mud in their buildings. The flood also knocked out power lines and gasoline pumps and sent propane tanks floating through town, polluting the lakes and streams.

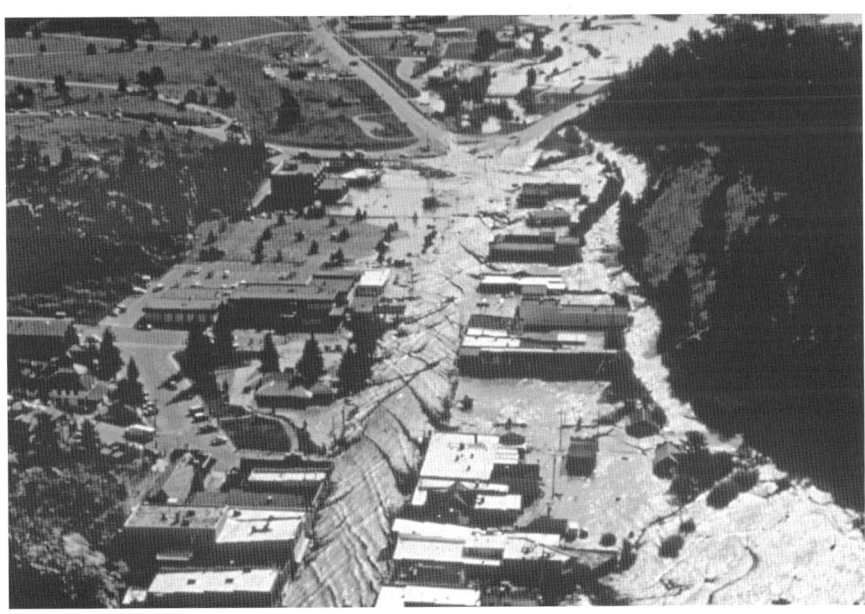

Estes Park, Colorado Dam collapse and flood, photo taken in July 1982. *U.S. Geological Survey*.

## Colorado's Deadliest Floods

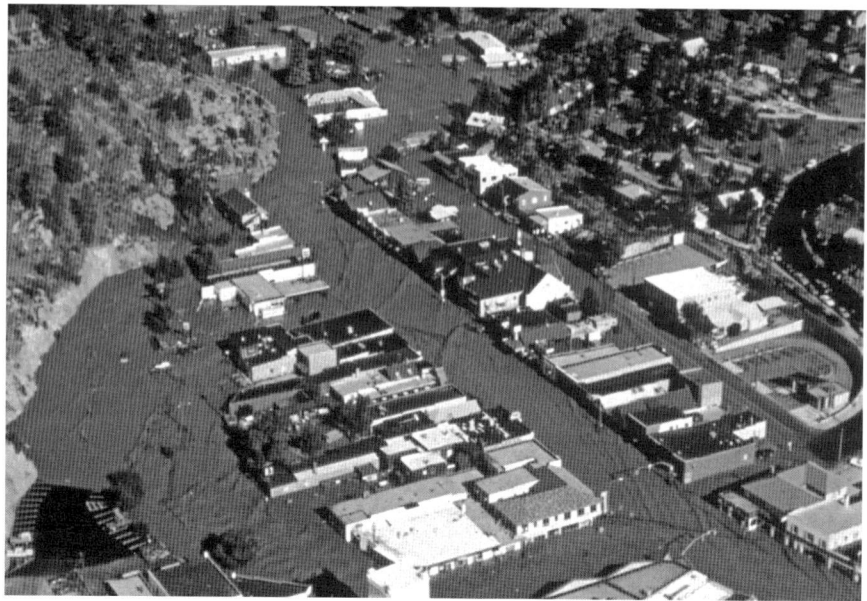

Looking upstream at the west end of Estes Park during the peak flow of the flood of July 15, 1982, caused by failures of Lawn Lake Dam and Cascade Lake Dam. *U.S. Geological Survey.*

When the flooding stopped, it was determined that eighteen bridges were damaged and in need of repair. There were 177 businesses in Estes Park filled with between two and four feet of mud. There was flood and mud damage to 108 homes. The final flood damage was estimated at $46,500,000.

Governor Richard Lamm was not in Colorado at the time of the flood, so Lieutenant Governor Nancy Dick sent the National Guard to Estes Park. They were sent to assist the local police, as there were reports of looting (these reports were later discovered to be false). Three people died in the Lawn Lake Dam flood.

### THE ALLUVIAL FAN

One of the more fascinating aspects of the Lawn Lake Dam flood was the alluvial fan left behind when the 219 gallons of water poured through the Roaring River and widened its channel by ten feet. It also left debris consisting of sand and gravel at the base of the mountain, which formed the alluvial fan.

The alluvial fan is shaped like a triangle and covers 42.3 total acres. It also contains 364,000 cubic feet of debris, according to the National Park Service, or "enough to cover a football field to a depth of 205 feet." The park service estimates that the debris weighs 829,000 tons, all moved by the force of the water from the Roaring River, which also moved a 452-ton boulder. Debris from the flood also created a natural dam on Fall River, which in turn created a 17-acre lake near the alluvial fan.

## COLORADO'S DAMS

Florida's *Evening Independent* posted an interview with Hal Simpson of the State of Colorado Engineer's Office after the flood. Simpson called the Lawn Lake Dam a "moderate dam hazard" and admitted that it should have been inspected at least every other year, when in fact it had been so long since the last inspection that the road had completely disappeared.

Simpson also admitted that staff members were behind on their work, explaining that (in 1982) the agency only had seven inspectors to cover 2,200 dams in Colorado. The Lawn Lake Dam could only be reached by a six-mile hike up the mountainside.

Mary Karaker, a spokeswoman for Rocky Mountain National Park, told reporters that the reservoir was actually "full to overflowing" prior to the dam collapse with 800 feet of water, "enough to cover 800 acres one foot deep."

According to the USGS, over one hundred floods have occurred in Colorado, including the Lawn Lake Dam and the Cascade Lake Dam. The Lawn Lake Dam failure was important to Coloradoans—for the first time, the government admitted that dams were not inspected the way they should be in the state. It was revealed that 1982 inspection reports of Bluebird Dam, Pear Lake Dam and Sand Beach Dam showed the dams were "seriously deficient and posing a hazard to residents living below them." All three dams were located high up within Rocky Mountain National Park.

It was also revealed that the responsibility for the upkeep of these dams was not the National Park Service, but the City of Longmont. The city decided that the dams no longer served an important purpose after the creation of the Buttonrock Reservoir, so the dams were destroyed. Before they could be destroyed, however, Rocky Mountain National Park had to purchase them, for $3,926,794.89.

## 11

# THE SPRING CREEK FLOOD OF 1997

## THE NIGHT THE KITTEN ROARED

*Nothing is softer or more flexible than water, yet nothing can resist it.*
—*Lao Tzu*

Fort Collins is a college town in northern Colorado. Founded in 1864, it was originally used by the military to keep travelers safe as they moved west along the Overland Trail. It is the home of Colorado State University and has a large, transient, college-age population. According to an article in the *New York Times*, Fort Collins was one of two small towns used by Walt Disney as inspiration for the Main Street, U.S.A. entrances to Disneyland parks around the world.

Like many Colorado towns, Fort Collins is graced with a picturesque stream. Spring Creek is a tributary of the Cache La Poudre River. It originates north of Horsetooth Mountain and exits out of Spring Canyon Dam. Spring Creek quietly meanders through the most populated areas of town south of Colorado State University and is bordered by a popular six-mile walking trail that goes under numerous road bridges.

Residents who used the trail referred to Spring Creek as more of a trickle than a stream, with a bed five feet wide, sometimes less in places. The sound of water sliding smoothly over rocks was like the purr of a kitten. On the night of July 28, 1997, the kitten roared.

## THE STORM

It was hot and dry for six weeks, which is not surprising for Colorado in July, though longtime residents remember the days when the weather was predictable, when children played hard in the morning because they knew the afternoon thunderstorms rolled in near lunchtime and the rest of the day would be spent inside. These were particularly dry times, though, and unusually hot. Something felt out of place. The heat created a drought, and residents were concerned about wildfires. Meteorologists started comparing the weather patterns that summer to those that sparked the Big Thompson Flood.

Meanwhile, an El Niño event was taking place in the Pacific. In *The Colorado Weather Book*, meteorologist Mike Nelson discusses El Niños and their influence on winter weather in Colorado. But this particular event was strong enough to effect the summertime weather, as well. Colorado also experiences a southern wind pattern in July that Nelson refers to as a "monsoon flow." When the monsoon flow combined with the El Nino, rain fell almost daily.

On July 27, 1997, the western portion of Fort Collins and nearby LaPorte had small storms that brought big rains. There were reports of flooding in areas of low population. There was rain throughout Fort Collins, but it was varied—heavy in some places and light in others. As night came, the rains increased.

On July 28, the residents of Fort Collins and surrounding areas awoke to pouring rain, particularly near the Foothills. From Horsetooth Reservoir north there was an additional ten inches before noon. South and southwest Fort Collins had an additional four inches. The ground was saturated, which is always a dangerous sign.

When the rain began to ease up in the early afternoon hours, meteorologists sighed with relief, but that feeling didn't last long. At 6:00 p.m., Fort Collins was hit with sheets of rain pouring thick and fast on the city, dumping more rain than was ever recorded in an urban area of Colorado. Over a two-day, thirty-hour period, 14.5 inches of rainwater flowed into the Spring Creek watershed on the western half of the city of Fort Collins—10 inches in six hours alone. It was the beginning of a nightmare.

Flooding was so immediate and rescue efforts so disjointed that the flood is now used to train emergency responders about worst-case scenarios. The Colorado State Police Department's emergency facility flooded. Many responders didn't know what was happening or where to go. In addition to the Spring Creek flooding, there was so much water on Remington, Elizabeth and Shields Streets that these roads looked like rivers.

The flood at Spring Creek was a shock to everyone, particularly emergency responders who were unable to communicate with administrators and lacked information about the areas affected by the flood as well as the extent of flooding. The city manager was unaware of the flooding on College Avenue and Remington Street and even farther north. According to NOAA, "When the city manager arrived at the Police Department's Command Center, everything was in turmoil." The city was in total chaos.

I recall watching television when the screen went black and a voice said, "If you are trying to call 911, we are aware there is an emergency and will get to you as quickly as we can," then the show returned. But they never said what type of emergency it was. All I could do was call my children and tell them to stay where they were. I didn't know what was happening until I looked out my front door and realized the entire street was flooded.

## THE TRAIN

The ground was saturated and the storm water had no place to go but forward. It moved into a drainage basin beneath a railroad bridge. The railroad bed became the focal point of the flood. The bed took on the function of an earthen dam, guiding the water to the railroad bridge, but the opening wasn't wide enough, and the flooding was instantaneous.

A moving freight train was crossing near Prospect Road and College Avenue in the heart of Fort Collins. The train derailed and ruptured a natural gas line, in the process creating an explosion that destroyed many local businesses. Emergency responders had no way of knowing what was on the train and if it posed larger threats to the city.

The flooding around the railroad bridge continued to build. A nearby clogged culvert let loose, and the water pressure created a flash flood waterwall that slammed into a mobile home park near Spring Creek.

## THE MOBILE HOME PARK

Colorado resident CarolJoy Collins lived in a two-bedroom trailer in one of two adjacent trailer parks near Spring Creek with her dachshund, two cats and four rabbits. The trailer parks had ninety homes stretched between College Avenue and the fifteen-foot-high bank that held the Burlington Northern Railroad tracks. Collins, who didn't own a television, monitored the weather with her radio. She knew there was flooding. She heard an announcement that the floods were taking place near the town of Laporte, but she had to work early the next morning. Laporte is far enough away from Fort Collins that many residents were left with a false sense of safety.

Those who did have televisions saw the screen go black earlier in the afternoon. Clearly, a disaster of some kind was taking place, but the type and extent of the emergency wasn't clear to anyone, not even the police department, fire department and other emergency responders.

Collins didn't hear a television announcement, but she did hear the rain. Regardless of the distance between her home and Laporte, there was something in the storm that made her suspect there might be possible dangers. However, she did have to work early the next day at her job at a nearby McDonald's restaurant, where she had been employed for twenty-two years. She was reliable, dependable and never late. She needed her rest…but decided to check the radio reports one more time.

As Collins recalls, according to the radio report at 9:30 p.m., the floodwaters were near a popular historic gas station and convenience store named Ted's Place, located at the intersection of Highway 287 and Highway 14. This was also known as the entrance to the tourist drive into the Poudre Canyon. It was miles away, north of town. Collins decided to go to bed, unaware of a failure in the emergency communications in Fort Collins and unaware that she was already in serious danger.

Collins was drifting off to sleep when she suddenly heard a scream. She sat up in bed, confused, unsure of what she had just heard. Then it came again. And again. People were screaming outside of her home.

Collins looked at the clock. It was 10:15 p.m. Still groggy, she climbed out of bed. The floors were dry. She walked to the front door and looked outside. There was three feet of water on the ground. Collins placed her Dachshund, Maximillian, in his kennel. She lifted her four rabbits from their hutches and placed them in another kennel. She grabbed her purse.

When Collins opened the door and stepped onto her front porch, she felt the porch crashing into the water and took a step back. She stared out into the darkness and saw flames. She heard more screams. She watched in shock as her car floated past her house. In one swift move, she turned her body and tossed the dog and rabbit kennels back into the house then felt herself falling. She grabbed the screen door and felt her body continue to move. Her entire home was moving, and she was dragged along with it. Her home was floating in the creek.

Collins continued to cling to the handle of her screen door. Her house floated around a tree and hit a vehicle, then another trailer home, almost knocking her from the door. "All I could think about was how to get back inside the house," she said. "I was praying for God to pick me up and put me back inside." Finally, the house wedged against a tree and the door swung back toward the house. Collins climbed back inside.

Once inside, she discovered that there was three feet of water on her floors. "I knew I had lost some of my pets," she said. "It had to have happened." Her favorite English Angora rabbit and chocolate rabbit were killed.

Collins looked out the door and saw lights. She recognized the lights and realized her home was completely turned around and tilted at an angle. She placed the remaining rabbits in a cage and begged them not to fight with each other. "I don't want you to die," she remembers telling them.

Then she heard shouting from the front of her home. A man's voice said, "If you're in your house please open your door and wave so we know where you are!"

Collins quickly opened the door and waved to a man in a boat. She saw a skunk floating past her. Her first instinct was to reach down and save it, but she realized she couldn't. The man came closer and helped her into

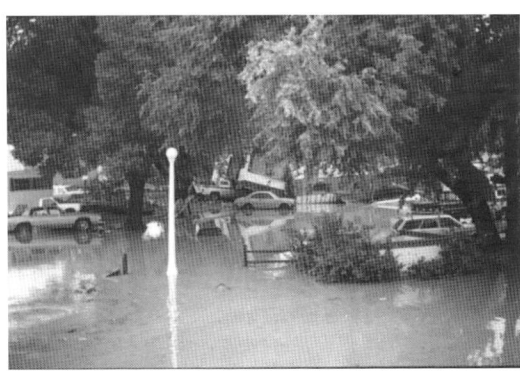

Damage from the 1997 Spring Creek Flood. *Courtesy of Colorado Department of Natural Resources.*

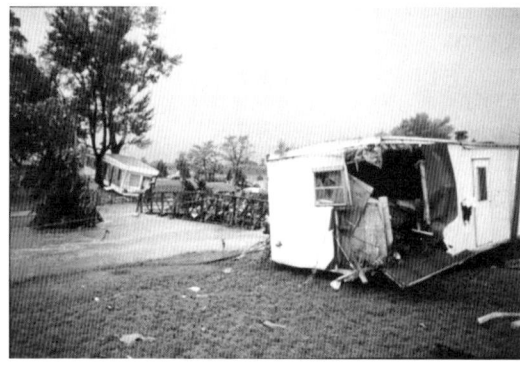

Trailer homes damaged in the 1997 Spring Creek Flood. *Courtesy of Colorado Department of Natural Resources.*

the boat. She took her dog but was forced to leave her rabbits behind, along with two cats that she couldn't find. She remembers a young boy in the boat who was terrified and screaming, so she let him pet her dog so he would stay calm.

Collins was in shock. She could not believe how much water was around her. It was difficult to understand what was happening in the dark. She knew she had just been rescued by the fire department. She recognized some of her neighbors standing on high ground. After she was helped from the boat, she was taken to what was then an Arby's restaurant.

Collins was thrilled to find more of her neighbors, then learned the terrible news—her next-door neighbor, JoAnn Roth, had drowned. Roth was supposed to babysit her one-year-old and three-year-old grandchildren that night, but plans had been changed at the last minute. Roth and her husband, Ronald, were swept into the floodwaters. Ronald was holding on to a tree and trying to hold on to his wife at the same time when the waters tore JoAnn from his grasp.

Rusty Golden lived near Drake Road at the time of the flood. When he realized the park was flooding, he tried to call his wife, who was with her cousin. When he reached her, he told her to stay in a safe place, then he searched for a way out of the park. The only path he could find was behind a gas station and near the railroad tracks.

As he moved through the water, Golden recognized a man he knew only as Rosendo. The man and his brother were using a garden hose to rescue people from their homes. "They eventually tied the hose to me and we made a human chain, like a train. I was like an anchor," Golden said. "The two men would swim out with a life vest, put it on a person then pull them back along the garden hose. One person snagged on a barbed wire fence. Once we got him over that, the guys went back for another."

"We spotted a man standing on a doghouse," Golden continued. "I thought it was strange because he wasn't calling out, then someone yelled to us that he was a deaf mute. They shouted, 'Oh my God, help him!' and Rosendo swam out to him."

"I can certainly tell you what it is like to have a train wash out ten feet away from you," Golden said. "We were standing next to it when the water took it out. I can still see things from that night. I can still hear the waters and the voices of the people. I had to yell at an elderly woman to get back in the window of her trailer for her safety." The garden hose that was used to perform rescues is now on display at a local museum.

## COLORADO STATE UNIVERSITY'S MORGAN LIBRARY

Colorado State University's Morgan Library was in the process of a remodel in 1997. The staff moved most of a large number of books into the basement—a total of nearly 500,000 volumes, including the library's entire bound journal collection and most of the sciences, social sciences and humanities collections, according to the university's library website.

When the flood hit, the basement filled with eight feet of water. Most of the books were destroyed, not just by the floodwater but also by the raw sewage that was released into the seven-foot wall of water that slammed into the university's campus. (The website also states that this was the third-largest library disaster in the history of the United States, behind the disasters that occurred during the Katrina and Rita hurricanes.)

There was a tremendous response from neighboring libraries, restoration specialists and the public to help restore the Morgan Library. More than one hundred people were needed to pack the seventy thousand boxes of mushy paper, which were loaded onto pallets. The pallets were stacked in refrigerated tractor trailers filled with liquid nitrogen, then the documents, books and journals were sent to a freezing facility in Fort Worth, Texas. The journals, documents and books were then sorted a second time to determine if they could be saved. They also had to be thawed and cleansed before freeze-drying, a costly and time-consuming process.

The basement of the Morgan Library had to be remodeled, as well. The shelving and floors were fairly new, but they were flooded with raw sewage and there was nothing that could be done to salvage or repair them. They needed to be completely replaced.

It was a particularly hot summer that year, and the heat created a fast-growing mold that appeared within three days and spread throughout the basement and threatened to destroy what was left of the library's collection on the upper levels. The mold was also destroyed at great expense.

It was ten years before the Morgan Library was completely restored so that the salvaged collection could be re-catalogued or replaced. Through the disaster, the library became a role model for emergency library recovery with its programs of interlibrary loan, electronic service, information literacy education and disaster preparedness. The landscaping around the library was also changed to help mitigate potential flood damage.

It is estimated that the total cost to repair the damage to the Morgan Library was $12,750,000. The 1997 flood was the fifth in Fort Collins to affect Colorado State University. The campus also flooded in 1902, 1938, 1951 and 1992.

## THE STREETS OF FORT COLLINS

Before darkness fell, many residents could see fields and the lawns at the university form into lakes. Gutters were already filled with debris, and this was part of the problem. The drains in the city were blocked. The streets became raging rivers. Within a matter of minutes, residents were struggling to survive the floodwaters, particularly those people living on Remington Street across from the CSU campus.

Robert Bunnell lived on Remington Street at the time. He recalls standing on the front porch of his home and staring at the house directly across the street. "I could see nothing but water from porch to porch," he said. "I think that's what shocked me the most. It was like a river flowing down the middle of the road."

Michelle Levine also lived on Remington Street in 1997. She was in Loveland with her father and stepmother on the day of the flood. Her stepmother, a dispatcher for the Loveland Police Department, was called in to work, and Levine went with her.

Levine recalls a tremendous amount of confusion, primarily over the large number of frantic, panicked callers who were redirected to Loveland from Fort Collins because their calls were not picked up at the Fort Collins dispatch center. The dispatchers in Loveland didn't understand what was happening. In fact, it wasn't until the next day that most of them discovered there was a flood in Fort Collins. All they knew at the time was that there were too many emergency phone calls—no one could track what was happening.

"I don't think anyone understood how badly it had flooded," Levine explained. "When you said flooding, to me, at that time, that meant the streets were flooded and we shouldn't be driving. I don't think anyone understood that trailer homes were washing down a raging river in the center of town!"

"I remember playing in the creek as a kid," Levine continued. "My friends and I would fish for crawdads. The deepest I ever recall the water was near the bottom of my ankles. It was a place where we felt safe playing without asking for adult supervision. There was no reason to have adult supervision. Honestly, I would allow my kids to play in it now if it wasn't for the memories of the flood. Even now if you walk through the park and look at it you see a trickle of water, a creek."

The trickle had become a massive flood. On the north side of town, students leaving a popular hamburger restaurant/bar were leaping into the water and sliding down the streets while police officers tried to pull them out. On the south end of town, in the two adjacent trailer parks, people were screaming for help, climbing into trees, clinging to their loved ones and dying in the floodwater while neighbors tried desperately to save them.

Joshuah Agnew was a student at Fort Collins High School and a member of the school's football team. He was with his fellow team members at a house on the south side of Spring Creek. His home was on the north side of the creek. Agnew, who was driving his mother's low-profile car at the time, decided to go home and check on his mother. "I don't remember it as an emergency," he said. "I was just going home."

In order to reach his home, Agnew had to cross the Remington Street Bridge, which was washed out by the wall of water a short time later. "The threat didn't seem as intense where I was at the time," he explained. "We were on high ground [at my friend's house] closer to Drake and College. I don't think I realized how much danger I was in until I was at home and saw what was happening on the news."

"I was nervous driving down Remington Street," Agnew recalls. "I got onto Remington closer to Elizabeth. Before that, the water didn't seem as deep, then I got home and realized the car was floating. The car floated into the driveway. I lost control of the car once I turned into the driveway and I realized the water carried me in at that point. The next day I went back with friends to the Spring Creek area to see for myself. I could see trees that were uprooted and cars that had floated away. It wasn't until I moved to Texas and flooding became much more frequent that I began to respect the danger of high water."

Danny Burd and his friend, Bruce, knew it was raining hard, but they didn't know the streets were flooded until they reached Elizabeth. "Bruce was driving," Burd explained. "Bruce lived right by that Baptist church, by Circle K [convenience store]. After crossing Elizabeth and seeing the next street even more flooded, we tried to turn around through the neighborhood. We are the type to have a cool head in bad situations, but it was scary. We locked arms and got out. We saw cars hydroplaning, a lot of cars stalled in the street, debris floating down the streets and in the river." Burd said he saw trees floating past, along with tires and trash. "And, of course we saw college kids tubing down the streets, too," he said.

## THE DAY AFTER AND RECOVERY EFFORTS

The day after the flood, Bunnell recalls walking down streets and alleys and seeing appliances and household items smashed, destroyed and in piles as if they were washed out of homes. A year later, he tried to purchase a home in the same area. Many of the homes had cracks in the foundation, and he could still see the water line on some, but it was the city's drainage system he remembers the most, and the extensive work required to repair the damage to the streets.

Michelle Levine was also curious about the flood and walked along the trail with her stepmother.

> *We walked along the Spring Creek walking trail near the creek. The trail crossed over by where the Fort Collins Pulse once was, and that was where we started to see the damage. The 7-11 store was completely washed out. The liquor store nearby was washed out. Entire buildings were destroyed. We saw pieces of houses and walls in the river.*
>
> *This was my first experience with a flood. I didn't think about the danger. We didn't even know yet that people were missing, or had died. We did know to stay out of the water, but we didn't know how serious it was until a police officer shouted to us that people were still missing and we needed to stay away from the water. I didn't know how bad it was until I returned home to Fort Collins later that day and watched the news.*

*I still can't believe this is the same place where I used to fish for crawdads as a kid. The water wasn't even up to my ankles as a child. It was slow-moving, a place where children played without supervision. Honestly, I would have allowed my children to play in Spring Creek. Even now when I go back to look at it, it's just a creek.*

## LOSSES AND LESSONS LEARNED

There was a second flood the following day, when thirteen inches of rain fell near Pawnee Creek in Sterling, causing even more damage from flash floods.

During the Spring Creek Flood of July 27–28, 1997, five residents were killed by flash floods. All of the victims were women—JoAnn Roth, Rose Marie Rodriquez, Estefana Guarneros, Sarah Payne and Cindy Schulz. There were more than sixty-two injuries and $250 million in property damage.

The trauma of the Spring Creek Flood also inspired new approaches to monitoring weather, including a national weather-watch program called CoCoRaHS—Collaborative Rain, Hail and Snow Network. The program relies on volunteers to report measurements of rain, hail and snow. There is now a CoCoRaHS station set up at the White House, as well.

# 12
# MASS EVACUATIONS

## THE 2013 COLORADO FLOODS

*There are no greater treasures than the highest human qualities such as compassion, courage and hope. Not even tragic accident or disaster can destroy such treasures of the heart.*
—Daisaku Ikeda

When the rain started to fall on September 9, 2013, it certainly wasn't cause for alarm. It was early fall, the children returned to school, the leaves were starting to change…and the weather changed, too.

The problem began with a slow-moving cold front that stalled, which happens often in Colorado. But in this case, the cold front covered most of the eastern portion of Colorado. A warm, wet monsoon moved up from the south with rains that were fast and furious, causing catastrophic floods that reached from Colorado Springs to Fort Collins, from Estes Park and Boulder to Greeley and Fort Morgan.

The rain continued and intensified. On September 12, Boulder County was swimming in an additional 9.08 inches. And the rain continued to fall. The floods spread, as well, from Pikes Peak to Wyoming, swamping eighteen counties in Colorado. Northern Colorado took the brunt of the storm with massive floods in Larimer, Boulder and Weld Counties. Rainfall records were set and broken in six major rivers and their tributaries, with residents of at least a dozen cities fighting to survive or waiting for evacuations. Some meteorologists called it the worst flooding in five hundred years.

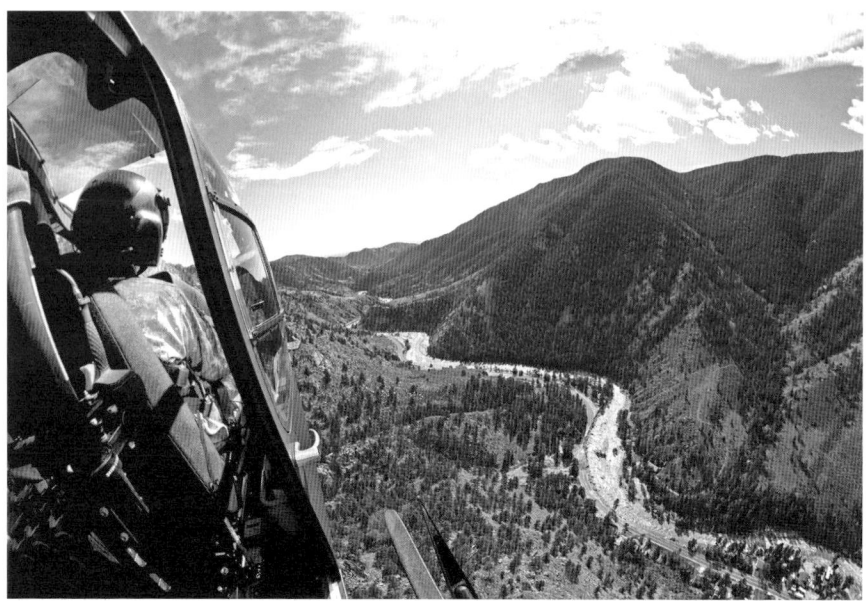

Chief Warrant Officer Troy Parmley, Colorado Army National Guard, checks floodwater levels. Colorado Guard members evacuated approximately 2,394 survivors. *U.S. Army photo by Sergeant First Class Jon Soucy.*

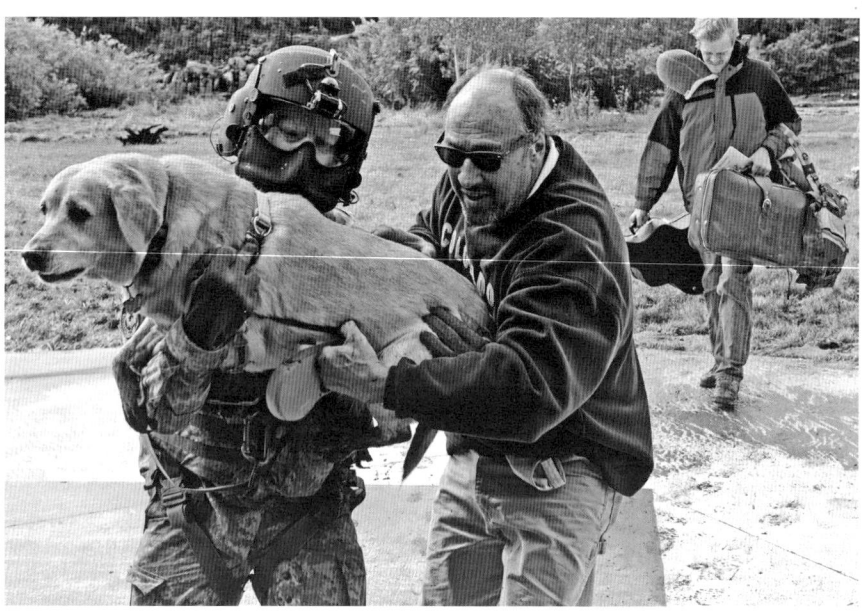

U.S. Army Sergeant Keith Bart carries a dog to safety in Boulder during the September 16, 2013 Colorado Floods. *U.S. Army photo by Sergeant Jonathan C. Thibault.*

To survive this storm, the people of Colorado would need assistance from everyone who could help, and they did help. This is the story of an appeal to all Americans for help and of their tremendous response. It is the story of a mass evacuation beyond description. It is a story of survival.

## BOULDER COUNTY

There's always something strange about the weather before a catastrophic flood occurs. In Boulder County, the strange event was record-breaking heat. It was ninety-three degrees on September 7, and students returning to classes at the University of Colorado wore sandals and shorts, and they sighed with relief when they heard rain was on the horizon.

When most people hear the words "cold front," they think of cool evenings sitting on the front porch watching the sunset. But cold fronts often stall over the Colorado Rocky Mountains, and stalling means floods. To a city like Boulder, stalled rainstorms are particularly dangerous. Boulder Creek flows through Boulder Canyon and down the center of the city of Boulder. It is peaceful and beautiful on an average summer day,

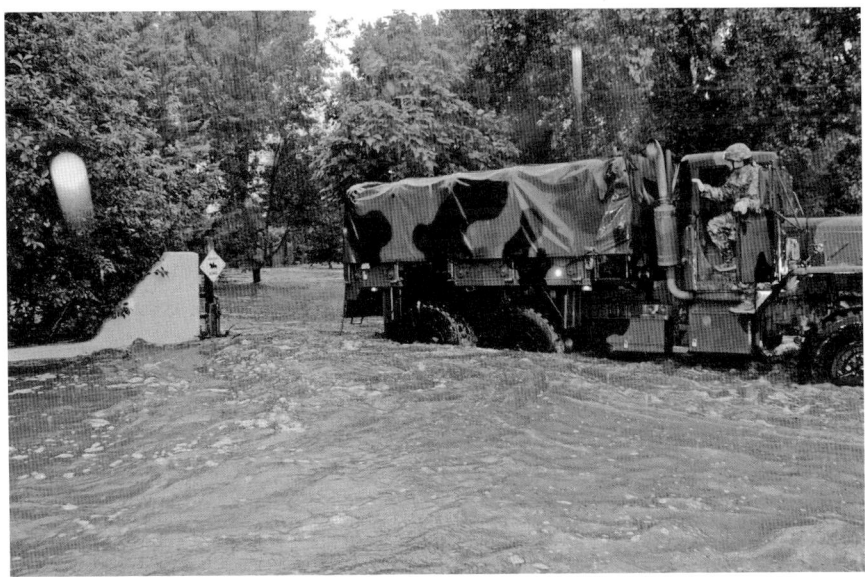

U.S. soldiers with the Colorado National Guard respond to floods in Boulder County during the Colorado Floods on September 12, 2013. *Department of Defense photo by Sergeant Joseph K. VonNida, U.S. Army National Guard.*

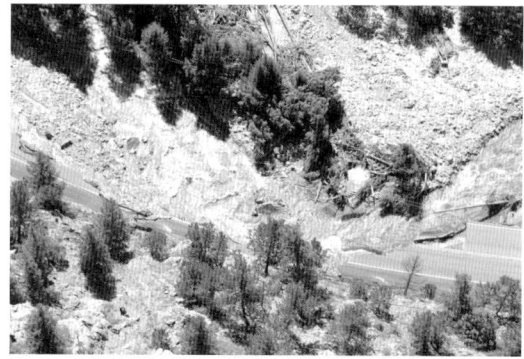

Aerial image of Boulder County taken on September 18, 2013, from a Colorado Army National Guard helicopter during the Colorado Floods of 2013. *U.S. Army National Guard photo by Staff Sergeant Jecca Geffre.*

but when a storm has stalled in the hills above town, the creek becomes an angry, raging beast destroying everything in its path.

Monday morning gave the deceptive appearance of another beautiful day, but by midafternoon the rains began to fall. Local firefighters watched the rain with concern. They had thirteen miles of scarred land from the Fourmile Fire in 2010, land with nothing in place to hold the water. An additional concern was prolonged periods of drought that had plagued Colorado for months. Land scarred by wildfires and dirt made crisp from the burning sun during periods of drought are also susceptible to flash floods, but emergency personnel were completely unaware that the rain they saw that day would bring floods beyond anything they could possibly imagine.

## LARIMER COUNTY

In Larimer County, five dams overflowed in Lyons, and the streets of Lyons, Boulder and Estes Park were flooded with water and mud. The flood was a shock to early-morning commuters who travel Highway 34 from Loveland to Estes Park. The road was washed out on September 11.

Many commuters were trapped in their vehicles when a long section of Highway 34 crashed into the Big Thompson River along with trucks and cars. Photos flashed across the morning news showing a mother and her child clinging to each other as they stood on top of her car; another photo showed a fireman trapped in a tree while National Guard members struggled with his rescue. There were three confirmed deaths, and one woman was missing. Her car was last seen rolling like a child's toy in the muddy water. An eighty-year-old woman was trapped in her Cedar Cove home as family raced to save her.

# Colorado's Deadliest Floods

## THE BIG THOMPSON FLOODS AGAIN

It was 10:24 a.m. when evacuation centers were announced for the Larimer County cities of Loveland, Lyons and Estes Park. A few hours later, at 12:30 p.m., the Larimer County Sheriff's Office ordered the evacuation of residents in and around the Big Thompson Canyon. Residents east of the collapsed section of road were sent to Loveland. Unfortunately, residents to the west were trapped by the broken highway and forced to drive back into Estes Park. Those residents who would need to cross bridges or dangerous sections of road were advised to stay in their homes and prepare to climb to high ground.

Around four o'clock in the afternoon, it was clear that residents of Lyons and Estes Park were stranded. Residents living between Buckhorn Road and Masonville were ordered to evacuate. A flash flood watch was issued in the Hyde Park area, which was also recovering from a forest fire. This watch was the first of many to come; initially, it attracted little attention. According to the National Weather Service, meteorologists expected a few inches of rain, but even that much can cause problems

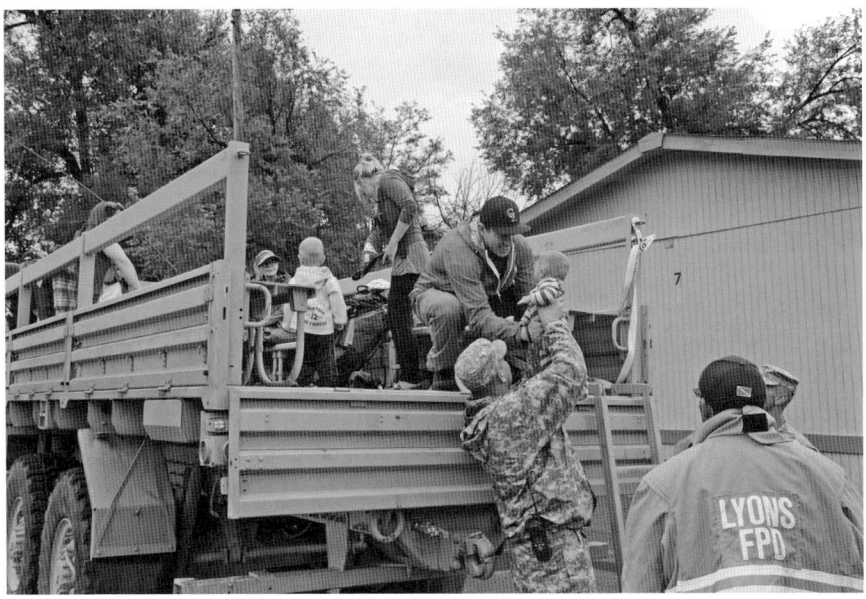

Colorado National Guardsmen transport evacuated residents of Lyons to Longmont on September 13, 2013, during the during the Colorado Floods. *Army National Guard Photo by Sergeant Joseph K. Von Nida.*

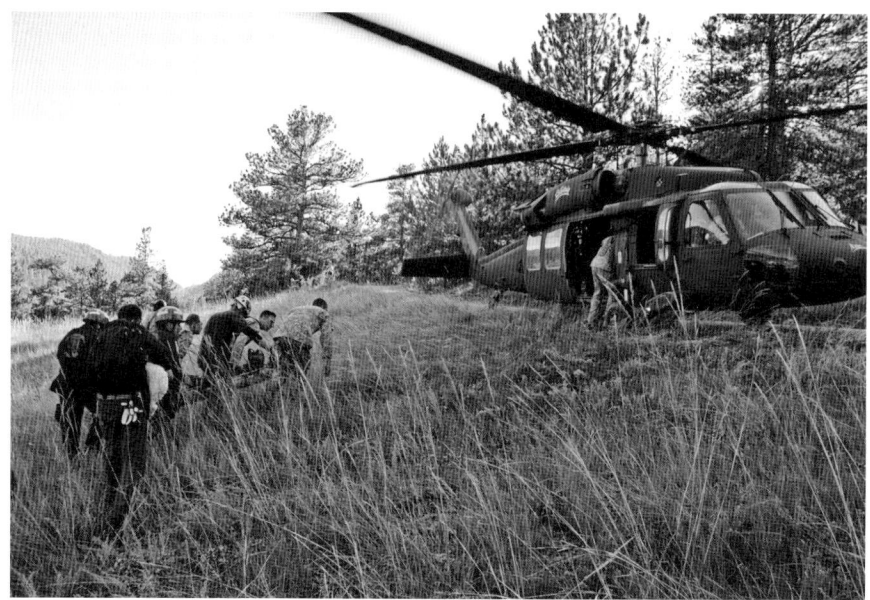

Civilian rescue personnel and U.S. soldiers with the Third Battalion, 157th Field Artillery Regiment, Colorado Army National Guard, use a rescue basket to load a flood evacuee on oxygen into a UH-60 Black Hawk helicopter assigned to the Second Battalion, 135th Aviation Regiment, on September 16, 2013, in Larimer County. *DoD photo by Sergeant Joseph K. VonNida, U.S. Army National Guard.*

in areas recovering from wildfires. Instead, the Hyde Park Area received eight inches, far more than it could handle.

Ulugbek Khudoynazarov is originally from Uzbekistan. He was living and working in Estes Park at the time of the flood. "I had been there for three months," Khudoynazarov said. "I had not seen this kind of flood before, because it may rain one or two days in Uzbekistan, but never much more."

Khudoynazarov worked at a local restaurant and was returning home from his shift on September 11, 2013, when he realized it was still raining, which meant it had been raining all day. He wasn't concerned until the next morning, though, when he woke up and discovered it had rained throughout the night.

"I prepared to go to work and on my way to the restaurant I discovered there was a flood in town," Khudoynazarov explained. He stopped to take photos then returned to the safety of his apartment. "I do not think I was in danger," he said. "If I was, I didn't realize it."

Unfortunately, Khudoynazarov had tickets to return home for a visit, and he was stuck in Estes Park because of the floods. "Both Highways 34 and 36 were closed so I couldn't get to the Denver airport for my flight," he said. I couldn't even contact the airlines because the phones were not working. I had to buy a new ticket and pay $200 for a ride to the airport because all shuttles and other transportation was not available.

"I had never seen so much water in town," Khudoynazarov continued. "I was shocked. It was very difficult for me. I had never even seen the stores close for a day!"

At the base of the canyon is Sunny Jim's Candy Ranch in Loveland. The candy store had been owned by Ida Suppress and her husband since 1964. Ida's husband passed away, and she now makes the candy and runs the store alone.

Suppress lives behind the store in a house that was built higher than the store and farther from the river with the intention of avoiding floods. Late in the evening on September 12, 2013, Suppress was notified that there was flooding in the canyon. She walked outside with a flashlight to check the water levels. She could see debris floating in the river.

The water seemed to be higher on the south side of the road. Suppress crossed the road and asked her elderly neighbor to join her to reduce the risks in case of evacuation. Suppress had been told by the Flood Plain Review Board that the water would have to rise at least seventeen feet to flood, so she felt somewhat secure. She decided to go to bed around 10:30 p.m.

It was close to midnight when she was awakened by the sound of something banging on the side of her house. Suppress ran to the windows and discovered that the banging sound was coming from debris. The Big Thompson River had flooded again, and it was right outside her door.

Suppress called to her two frightened dogs and moved them and her neighbor from across the street into the car, then helped her daughter and two more dogs into the car. They were walking in more than three feet of water. She was trying to drive her car onto Highway 34 when the floodwaters rose and started moving the vehicle back. That's when her neighbor started to scream. "I don't want to die! I don't want to die!"

Suppress tried to remain calm and control the vehicle. She realized the water was controlling her car. Suddenly, the tires hit a dry spot and grabbed on. The car moved forward up the hill. Her family, pets and neighbor were safe, but they had evacuated so quickly that they took nothing with them.

Suppress, her daughter and neighbor stayed at the homes of friends and family for weeks before they were allowed to return to check the damages. She could see that the water had been at least two and a half feet high when it hit the back of her house and at least ten feet high in her basement. Everything in her basement was destroyed, including all possessions she had in storage. This is the reality of flood recovery—her Christmas tree alone was worth $350.

In the candy store, all of the candy, supplies and ingredients were destroyed—Suppress had a chocolate delivery the day before the flood, and the loss of the candy alone exceeded $20,000. All carpet, sheetrock, tiles and anything near the floor was destroyed and had to be replaced. Suppress, her son, her daughter and volunteers had to wear suits and masks to protect themselves from the fumes coming from the floodwater, but it was vitally important that everything in her store and home be completely replaced and sterilized before she could pass inspection and open her store again. It took a lot of hard work, but Suppress succeeded. The total damages to her store and home is estimated at $245,000.

Randy Kady, a Loveland resident, works where Highway 34 entered the Big Thompson Canyon. He was able to make it into work on September 11 but spent the day watching the rain. "I would occasionally stream online one

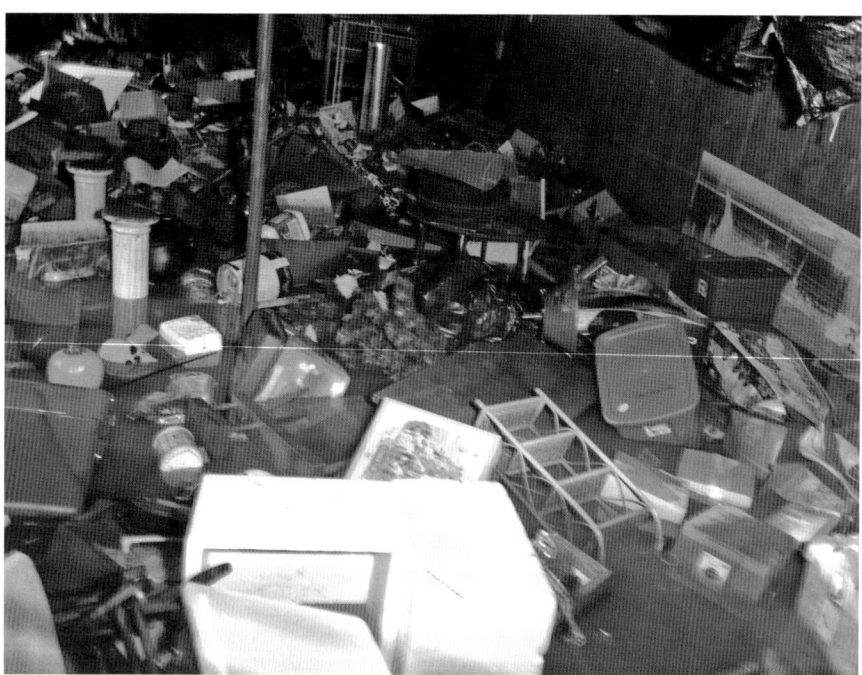

Basement of Ida Suppress following the 2013 Colorado Floods. *Photo by Bob Suppress.*

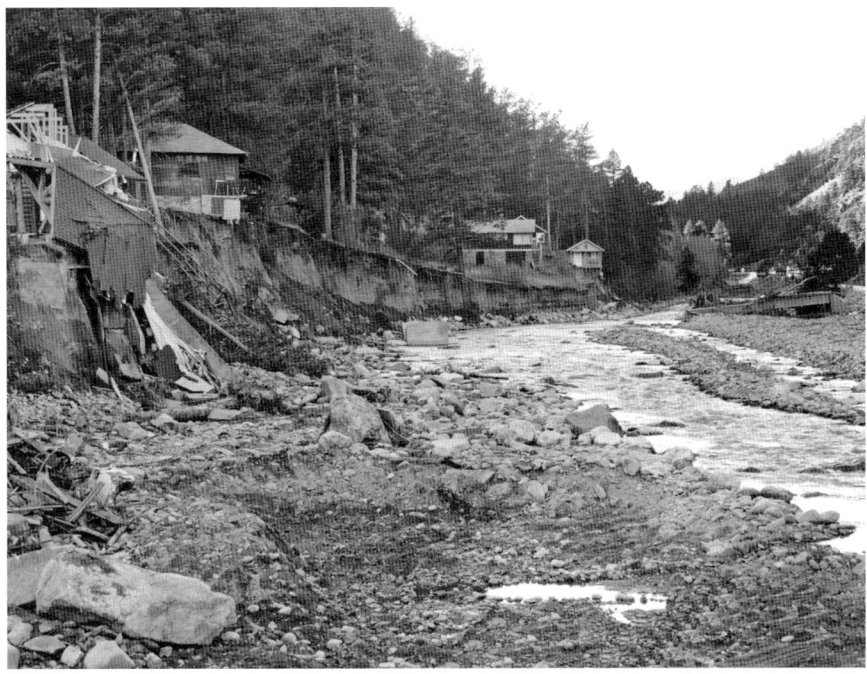

The house on the left hanging off the cliff belonged to the neighbor of Mary Myers of Drake, Colorado. Photo taken on September 13, 2013. *Courtesy of Mary Myers.*

of the news stations for updates," Kady said. "That is when I started to get a sense of how serious the flood was. I could see rain coming down in torrents just outside my window."

His daughter sent a text from her school around 10:45 a.m. asking him to pick her up and take her home. When he arrived at the school, he discovered that the police were already barricading sections near the river.

Kady first realized the flood might reach his home when he received an emergency alert on his phone at 2:00 a.m., September 12. Kady believes flooding is a very serious matter and stated that he would never ignore a warning or evacuation notice. He was a child of ten when the Big Thompson River flooded in 1976; the emergency notification reminded him of the fear and trauma when he heard about the canyon flood.

"I was up sick all night vomiting," Kady said, describing the trauma of learning what happened during the Big Thompson flood. Many local residents were reminded of the 1976 flood during the 2013 floods. "The devastation and loss of life was catastrophic," Kady said of the 1976 flood.

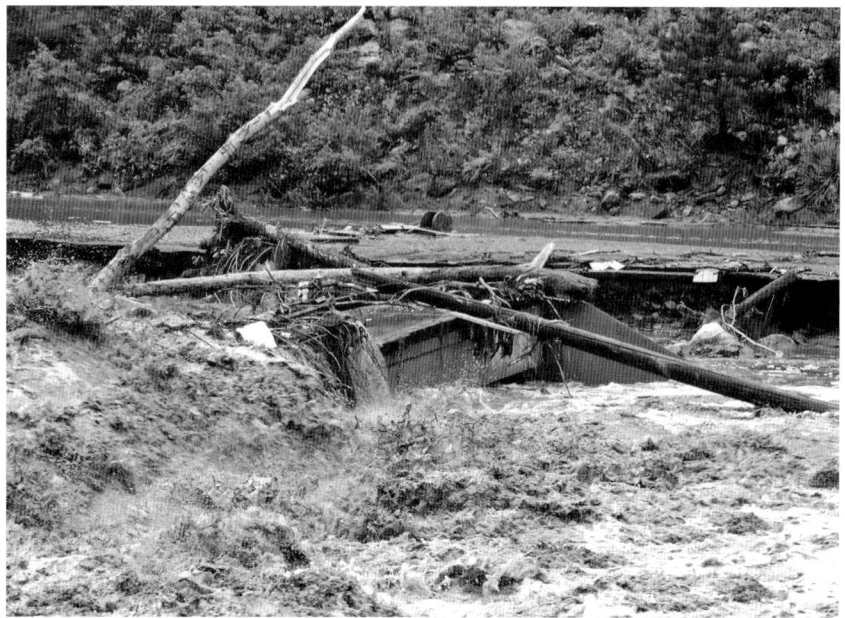

Moodie Bridge collapsed overnight and directed the Big Thompson River through the neighborhood. Photo taken on September 13, 2013. *Courtesy of Mary Myers, photographer. Drake, Colorado.*

In Larimer County, 1,120 square miles were flooded. A total of 1,500 homes and 200 businesses were destroyed by the floods, with 4,500 homes and 500 businesses reporting damaged. Due to the extensive road damage in the Big Thompson Canyon, the residents of Drake, Glen Haven and Cedar Park were trapped in their homes and on hillsides. Three dams collapsed. Fish Creek Road and all crossings were destroyed; people were trapped in their homes. The sewage lines were damaged, and raw sewage emptied into the Big Thompson River.

## FLOODS MAKE FAST CHANGES IN MOUNTAIN TOWNS

The first signs of trouble came in reports of problems with mud in Boulder. The first signs of danger came from Erie, where two police officers, responding to reports of flooding, became trapped by the floods. A transformer was on fire near the high school, and by 6:30 p.m., water was three feet deep in the streets.

# Colorado's Deadliest Floods

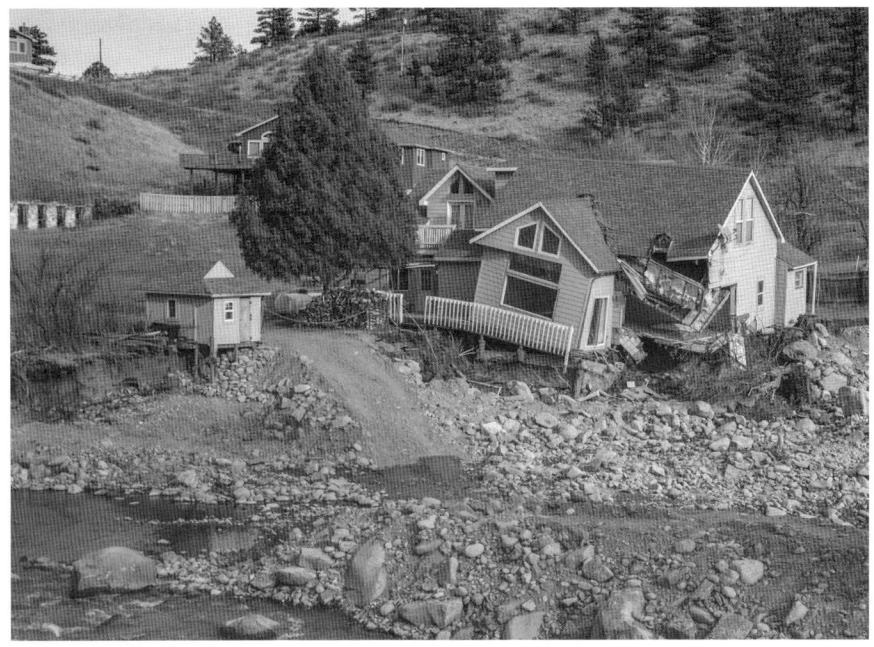

St. Vrain Canyon 2013 flood damage, two months later. *Photo by Flickr user Ed Ogle.*

By 8:00 p.m., Longmont's city manager, Harold Dominguez, had employees on the streets closing off the St. Vrain Beltway due to possible flooding. He had walked the road earlier and, acting on instinct and experience, made the decision to shut it down.

## DANGEROUS LESSONS FOR STUDENTS AT THE UNIVERSITY OF COLORADO

Back in Boulder, students at the University of Colorado, many of whom were unfamiliar with Colorado flash floods and the unpredictable weather, realized the water was high near campus. Instead of seeking shelter, they fetched inner tubes and were floating in the streets.

According to an article in the *Daily Camera*, students played "slip and slide" in a nearby field and used their inner tubes to float through tunnels designed for safe water flow during floods. The danger was building.

While the students played in the water, officials of the University of Colorado Boulder made calls to staff members asking for help in a growing emergency situation. Louise Vale, vice chancellor for administration at the University of Colorado Boulder, called the local police to warn them about the situation with the students. She then called the university's facilities management personnel to ask for assistance with monitoring the water situation. At 8:45 p.m., she sent an emergency text message to all university students and personnel, warning of possible flash floods and urging students and employees to avoid Boulder Creek.

The flood sirens in Boulder screamed their warning at 10:01 p.m. Minutes later, students were told to evacuate their dorms and move to higher ground. More than 380 students were evacuated.

It was a worst-case scenario come true for Boulder firefighters monitoring the Fourmile Fire burn, which was now being pounded with rain; all that rain flowed into Boulder Creek. Meanwhile, in the city, severe flooding was taking place at the Seventeenth, Eighteenth and Ninth and Twenty-Eighth Street Underpasses, Alpine Avenue, Manhatten Drive and Baseline and Foothills Parkways, two of the busiest streets in town.

Boulder was no longer under a flash flood watch; it was a warning. The flooding was there, and it was more than anyone could have imagined. The situation worsened by the minute as city employees struggled to control the danger, but that time had passed. They could see debris slamming into bridges, which meant the water had overflowed its banks and was moving with such power and strength that it was tearing up the landscape or, worse, tearing down homes and buildings.

By the next morning, September 12, Boulder Creek was flowing at five thousand cubic feet per second. Boulder County, where three people died, exceeded its yearly average of rainfall in this one storm. County officials evacuated 1,600 residents. There were 262 homes destroyed and 300 damaged. All told, nine hundred square miles of flooding occurred.

## NIGHTMARE IN JAMESTOWN

On September 12, a peaceful, environmental field trip in Jamestown quickly became a terrifying disaster. Little James Creek was no longer little as it came roaring down the mountainside, spreading so far from its banks that it was moving homes off their foundations.

Residents of Jamestown were ordered to evacuate, but many admitted later that they returned to their homes to check lights, close doors and retrieve possessions. Even more residents were at the elementary school digging trenches, trying to save the building.

Some never heard the evacuation warning. Joseph Howlett, seventy-two, was crushed beneath his own home. Howlett, a former business owner in Jamestown, was considered one of the town's patriarchs. His was the only death in Jamestown. Sadly, he was not found until six days later. Howlett was the first victim of the Colorado Floods of 2013. As his body was removed from his home, the townspeople stood outside and sang their goodbye.

The town was under siege, and Jamestown's mayor, Tara Schoedinger, was ready for battle, walking from home to home, banging on doors, insisting that residents evacuate immediately as the water raced down the mountain.

Jamestown was featured in national news. The town experienced complete devastation in spite of the valiant efforts of the residents who spent days cut off from rescuers due to the severity of the flooding. According to the Town of Jamestown's website, the area experienced intense flooding for three days straight; seventeen inches of rain fell in that time. It is estimated that Jamestown experienced $22 million in damages,

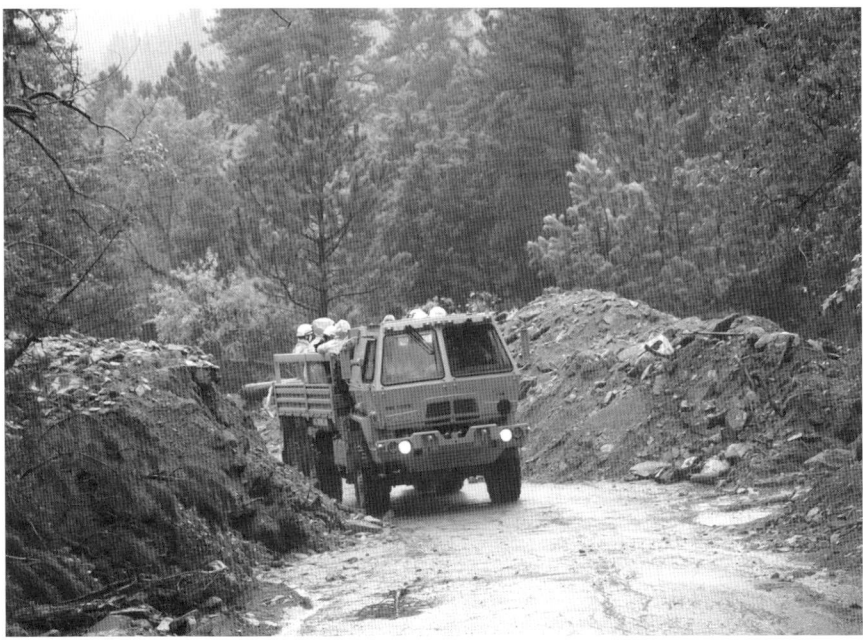

Nebraska Task Force One conducts search-and-rescue operations in the hard-hit mountain town of Jamestown during the Colorado Floods on September 15, 2013. *Photo by Michael Rieger, FEMA.*

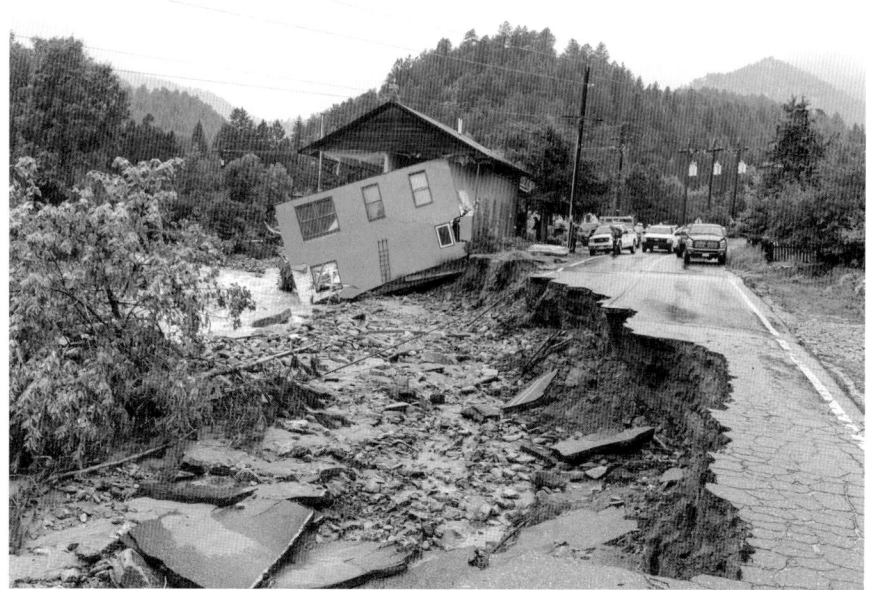

Jamestown, Colorado, was isolated by flooding from Boulder during the 2013 Colorado Floods. *Photo by Steve Zumwalt, FEMA.*

including eighteen destroyed homes and forty-four damaged homes and the loss of the Anderson Hill Bridge. The drinking-water plant was 50 percent destroyed, which greatly hindered the recovery process. The fire station was destroyed, the town square was destroyed and the post office was severely damaged. The elementary school was closed for the school year in spite of the valiant efforts of the people of the town. An estimated 90 percent of Jamestown residents were evacuated by helicopter and were homeless for months.

## THE FIELD TRIP

Expecting little more than light rain, four teachers and ten parents continued with their field trip plans, driving seventy-eight fifth-grade students from Fireside Elementary in Louisville to the Cal-Wood Education Center near Jamestown. This was no ordinary field trip. The teachers, parents and students planned three days of hiking and environmental education. When discussing Colorado's environment, these students were about to learn a lesson they would never forget. Little James Creek near Jamestown was rising fast to five times above its normal height.

The difference between two inches and eight is huge to a child in tiny shoes and a thin jacket. One of the teachers even lost her boots.

Parents and teachers quickly realized that the situation had turned desperate and moved the children to high ground, but they were cut off from communications with the parents of the rest of the children who no longer knew if their children had survived the flood. When the group was finally located, the news announced to the country that every member of the field trip had survived. They were rescued by the National Guard in seven Blackhawk helicopters.

## STATEWIDE FLOODING AND MASS EVACUATIONS

The statewide flood damage estimates and rain totals are staggering. The city of Aurora experienced flash floods after receiving 2.27 inches of rain in six hours. There was more flooding in Denver and surrounding areas, but possibly less damage. Denver received 3.72 inches of rain.

Fountain Creek once again flooded in El Paso County. Fort Carson had nineteen inches of rain. Colorado Springs lost one resident to the floods.

Jefferson County also reported severe flood damage in Coal Creek Canyon. Highway 72 was closed and did not reopen until November 2013. Evergreen was evacuated, and Bear Creek once again reached flood levels of nine feet.

The South Platte River also flooded again, at 11.2 feet, damaging seventy-three miles of asphalt and dirt roads in Logan County.

Goodrich, Orchard and Weldona in Morgan County were evacuated on September 14 when floodwaters reached thirteen feet.

The city of Evans in Weld County on the eastern plains had an average population of twenty thousand that varied due to the large number of immigrants working at the packing plants. Many of the residents were evacuated when the South Platte River overflowed. They returned home to find two feet of mud and water on their floors. In Weld County, the floods damaged 3,000 homes, 350 business and 2,377 crop fields. There was additional damage to bridges, and 654 miles of road were under water. The city of Greeley was evacuated; portions of Greeley also experienced severe flooding.

# Colorado's Deadliest Floods

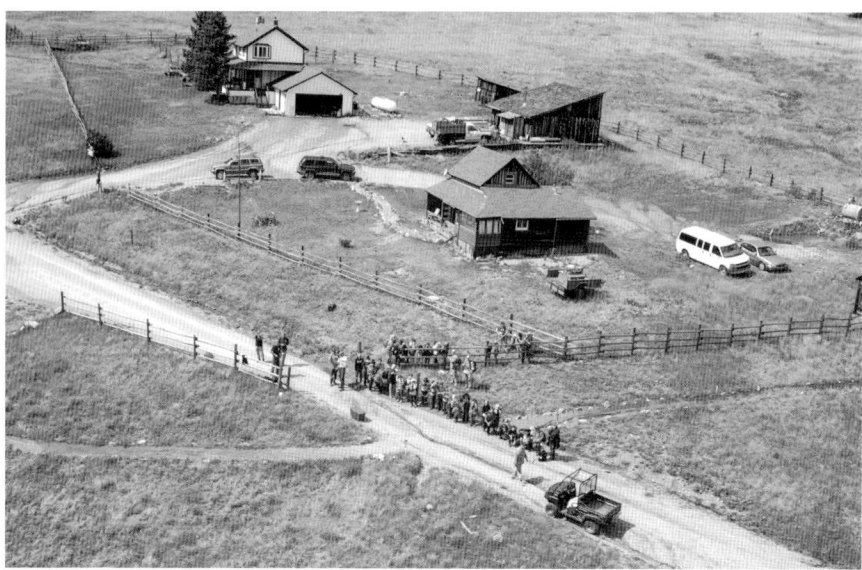

Soldiers out of Fort Carson and civilian rescue personnel rescue members of the Jamestown community and children from Cal-Wood Education Center during the Colorado Floods on September 14, 2013. *U.S. Air National Guard photo by Staff Sergeant Nicole Manzanare.*

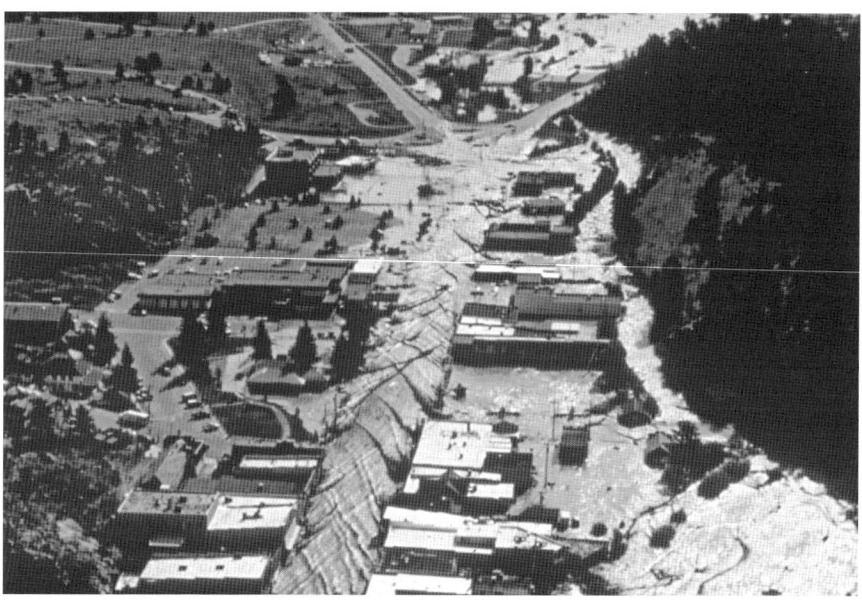

Roads were badly damaged in the Manitou Springs, Colorado area due to flooding. FEMA worked with local, state and other federal agencies to provide assistance to residents and business affected by the 2013 floods. *Photo by Patsy Lynch, FEMA.*

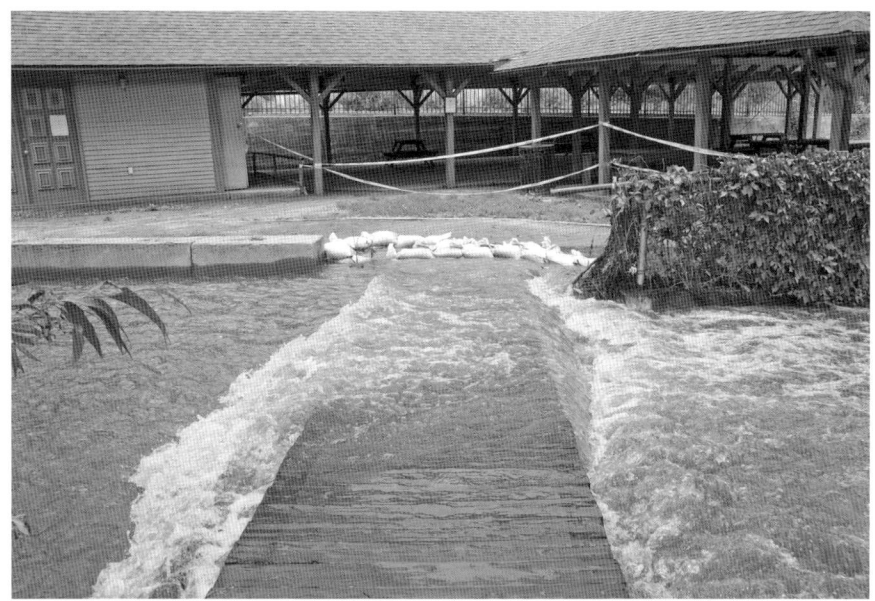

A small bridge is overwhelmed with water from the 2013 Colorado Floods. *Photo by Patsy Lynch, FEMA.*

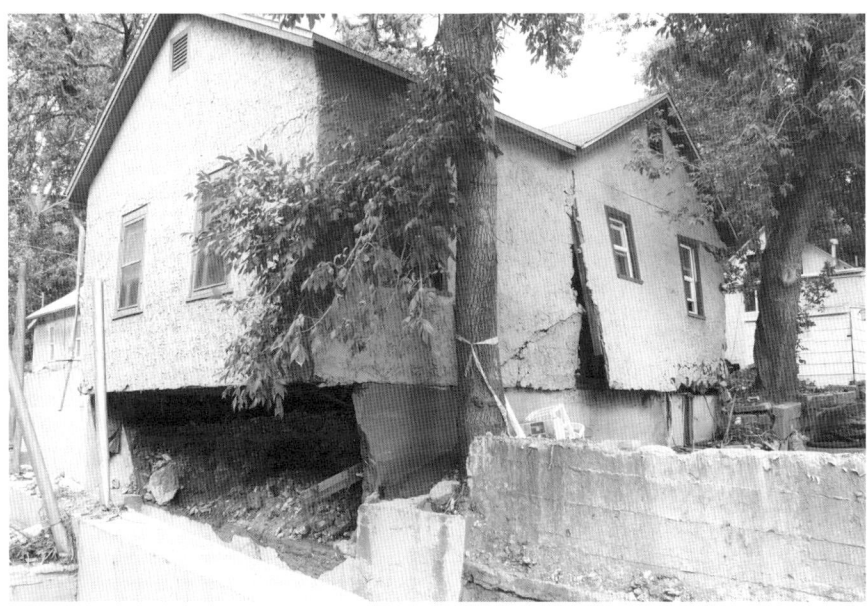

A home in Manitou Springs was badly damaged by floodwaters during the Colorado Floods of 2013. *Photo by Patsy Lynch, FEMA.*

# Colorado's Deadliest Floods

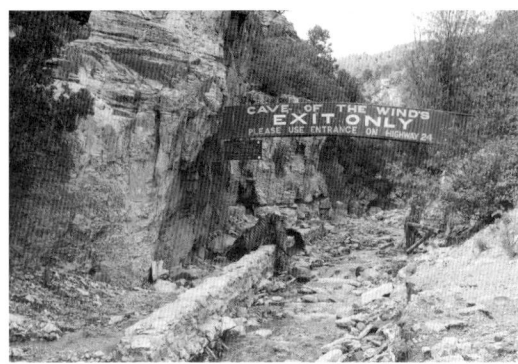

The road that led to Cave of the Winds in Manitou Springs was damaged by floodwaters in the 2013 Colorado Floods. *Photo by Patsy Lynch, FEMA.*

## ADDITIONAL DAMAGE AND LOSS ESTIMATES

Nine people died in the floods of 2013, which was truly shocking considering the huge number of evacuations and the widespread devastation. In addition to Mr. Howlett in Jamestown, there was a death in Cedar Creek; four people died in Boulder County; two died in El Paso County; and one was killed in Clear Creek County.

The Colorado Floods of 2013 are variously considered one-hundred-year, five-hundred-year and one-thousand-year floods. The Colorado cities most affected by flash floods and heavy rains include: Boulder, Jamestown, Lyons, Aurora, Brighton, Longmont, Estes Park, Denver (mostly on the east side), Fort Collins (mostly on the north side), Loveland, Commerce City, Eldorado Springs, Erie, Evans, Evergreen, Morrison, Milliken and Greeley. In the Foothills and eastern Colorado, flooding affected twenty-three counties, according to the National Weather Service.

It is estimated that the 2013 Colorado Floods damaged nineteen thousand houses, eight hundred commercial buildings, two hundred miles of roadway and twenty state highway bridges. The loss of crops and farmland is nearly impossible to estimate. Entire sections, some miles long, of train tracks were washed away in the floods, along with county roads, highways and, in places like Boulder and Fort Collins, city streets. Weld County, the largest county in the United States, lost 1,900 gas wells, closed off due to severe damage.

There is still concern that fluids from fracking in the city of Boulder and in Weld County may have been released in the floods. There is another concern that was fairly new to flood studies. Amy Pruden is a Virginia Tech environmental engineer. She pioneered the investigation of antibiotic resistance genes as environmental pollutants. After the floods of

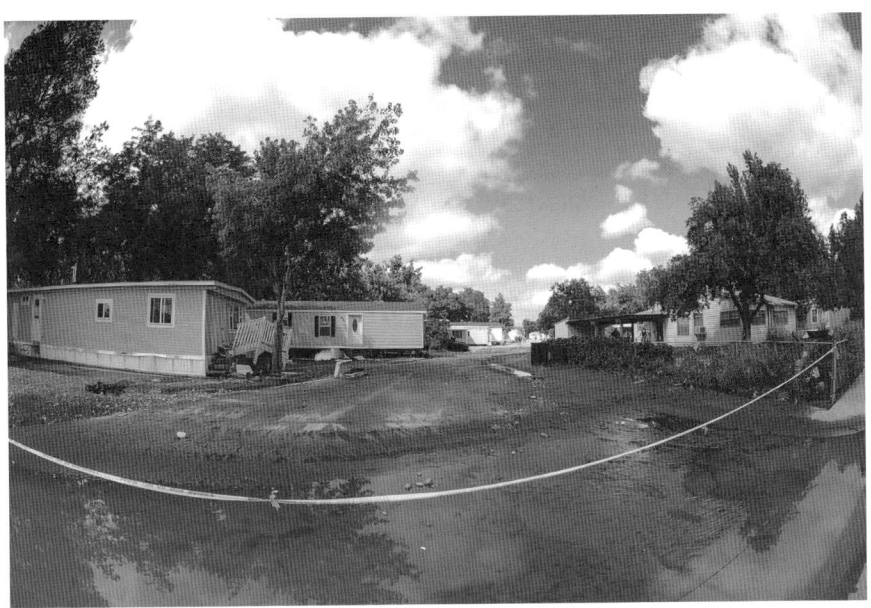

U.S. soldiers and airmen from the Colorado National Guard set up a checkpoint at a trailer park in Longmont during the Colorado Floods on September 16, 2013. *U.S. Air National Guard photo by Staff Sergeant Nicole Manzanares.*

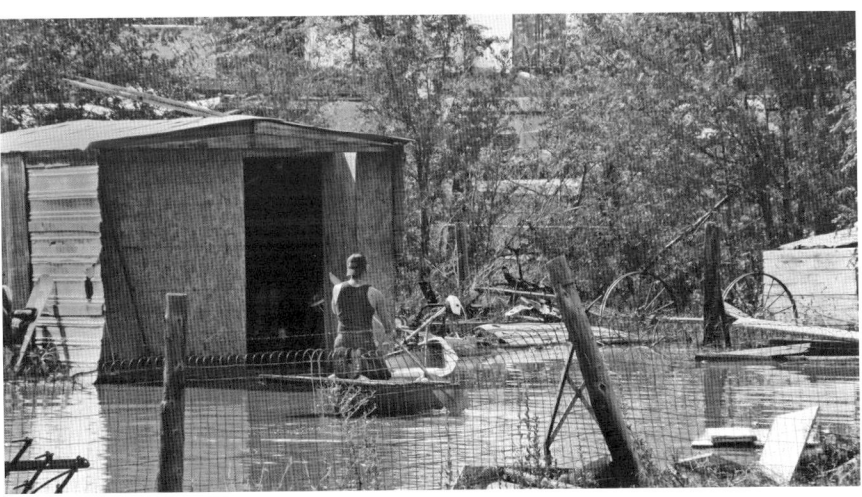

Man in kayak assessing the damage to his garage done by the 2013 Colorado Flood. *Photo by Lauryn McDowell available through Creative Commons license 2.0 attribution.*

2013, Pruden received a National Science Foundation (NSF) and a Rapid Response Research (RAPID) grant that enables her to study the effects of the 2013 Colorado Floods on antibiotic-resistance genes. She is working with Mazddak Arabi of Colorado State University and Diana Aga of the University of Buffalo, according to an article on Virginia Tech's website. The work is based on the theory that 90 percent of antibiotics pass through human bodies without metabolizing, which means these antibiotics are flushed into the water supply; during widespread floods, like the 2013 Colorado Floods, these antibiotics spread into the water supply statewide.

The damage estimate of this flood is challenging. It will take many years before an accurate total can be reached, but estimates in 2013 range from $1 to $2 billion.

## RECOVERY

Many communities took immediate action after the 2013 floods to mitigate the damages from repeat flooding. Boulder County started a buyout program to purchase properties that could possibly be damaged by future floods and leave the land undeveloped rather than allowing residents to rebuild.

After the two catastrophic floods and smaller floods, the Colorado Department of Transportation closed sections of Highway 34 leading into the Big Thompson Canyon in 2016 to repair and redesign the highway and river with the goal of mitigating future flood damage. The park built as a memorial to those who died in the 1976 Big Thompson Canyon Flood was destroyed and will be restored.

Nevertheless, some residents intend to remain in their homes by the river. Barb Anderson, cofounder of the Big Thompson Memorial, said:

> *People ask if we're going to get out of the canyon now, and I ask "Why?" This is our home and where we love to be. No, I am not leaving. When it is my time, I will go. In the 2013 floods, we knew in advance the flood was coming. We had a chance to leave, but chose to stay. This is when the protection instinct kicks in and you want to be as close to the place where you live without putting your life in danger. We were here for a purpose in both floods—to help others, which we did, and I don't regret it at all. Mother Nature has her own mind as to how things happen. God did not take those lives, Mother Nature did.*

# GLOSSARY

100 (500, ETC.) YEAR FLOOD: An odd term. No, it does not refer to a flood that occurs every one hundred years. According to historical data collected on floods in a certain area, the term means that a flood of a certain magnitude has a 1 percent chance of occurring in a given year.

100 (500, ETC.) YEAR STORM: According to historical data collected on rainfall, snowfall, etc., there is a 1 percent chance of a storm of a certain magnitude occurring in a given year.

ALLUVIAL FAN: Cone-shaped deposits of clay, silt, sand and gravel built up by streams or left after floods.

ALLUVIUM: Clay, silt, sand and gravel that is left, in the context of this book, after a flood and can contribute to particularly fertile soil.

ARROYO/WASH: A dry creek bed that fills with water during heavy rains or cloudbursts and can be very dangerous, especially for small children and animals.

CLOUDBURST FLOODS: Cloudbursts are extreme thunderstorms, often accompanied by hail, that either create flash floods or situations ripe for floods. According to numerous newspaper accounts accessed for documentation of facts in this book, in the mid- to late 1800s, residents of Colorado used the word "cloudburst" concurrently with "flash flood."

# Glossary

Cold front: This is the edge of a mass of cold air moving into an area. It is the "trailing edge" of a warm section of a low-pressure system.

Creek: Another term for a stream, also called a brook. Often underestimated, creeks can and will flood. They are generally connected to another stream or river.

Discharge/streamflow: The volume of water that is measured as it passes a certain point in a river in a determined amount of time and documented in cubic feet per second.

Drainage basin: A basin where rainwater or snowmelt collects at the low point, often the exit of the basin; water generally joins another body of water, such as a river or lake.

Dry gulch state: A difficult term to define, but it appears to be a slang term referring to V-shaped gulches that often remain dry due to droughts but can quickly fill with water during storms, creating potential flooding conditions.

El Niño/La Niña: According to Mike Nelson's *Colorado Weather Book*, the El Niño/La Niña is actually a pattern "that occurs every three to five years" and not a rare event as first suspected in the 1970s, when the pattern wreaked havoc on anchovy fishing, which in turn affected the poultry business (anchovies are often used in poultry feed).

Flash flood: A fast, sudden explosion of water that often arrives without warning and can visually appear to form a wall of water and debris.

Flood: A general term to describe any flow of water that moves over the top of its natural or artificial confinement.

Floodplain: Low-lying ground near a body of water; a particularly dangerous place to build a home. Homeowners who build on a floodplain are often unable to insure their homes.

Flood warning: A flood warning means that a flood is already occurring and it is time to seek shelter or, in the case of floods, find higher ground.

# Glossary

Flood watch: A watch means a flood may occur, that conditions are ripe for flooding. Residents should begin to prepare for a possible evacuation.

Headwater: The headwater is the place where something begins. During the 1976 Big Thompson Flood, rescuing officers searched for the headwater, or the source of the flooding, so that they could determine how far they had to drive to evacuate residents.

Hydrologist: Someone who studies bodies of water, including pollution, volume and soil samples.

Levee: Levees have many names, including dikes, embankments and floodbanks. They are generally built in an elongated shape following the natural shape of the surrounding landscape. They are often filled with earth and not particularly sturdy, especially during flood conditions.

Overland flood: Overland flooding occurs when floodwaters overflow banks and rise high enough to enter homes. Overland floods are particularly costly because many people do not realize that their standard household insurance does not cover flood damage.

Recurrence interval: This is an estimate of the average number of years between floods of a comparable size.

River: A river is a body of water larger than a stream that connects to another river and that flows into a lake or an ocean.

River stage: This is the measured height of water in a river.

Stalled Storm: A stationary storm, or front, that has little or slow forward movement.

Storm surge: A storm surge is seawater that rises and generally washes over land formations during atmospheric pressure changes and extreme winds that come with severe storms. The term has become more familiar since Hurricane Katrina, which had a storm surge of 27.8 feet, the highest storm surge recorded on a U.S. coast.

# Glossary

STREAM: A body of water lined by banks of mud or dirt that also has a current. Streams have many names, including branches, brooks and creeks.

SURFACE WATER: The top layer of a body of water or water collecting on a surface or on the ground. In flood situations, it is difficult to determine the speed and force of the water at first glance because the surface water may appear to be moving much slower than the water below it.

TRIBUTARIES: A tributary is a river or stream that flows into a larger river or lake, thus increasing the volume of water during storms and contributing to flood conditions.

UPSLOPE RAIN EVENT: An upslope rain event is much as it sounds—air flowing uphill expands and cools, thus forcing the moisture in the air to fall as rain.

WASHAWAYS: A washaway can be thought of as a landslide, but it is a particular type of landslide that generally occurs on embankments, bridges and structures created to support cars, trucks and trains.

# BIBLIOGRAPHY

*Alamosa Journal.* "Over One Hundred Lives Lost in Train Wreck Near Pueblo." August 12, 1904. http://www.kmitch.com/Pueblo/edenwreck.html.

Boulder County Colorado. "Boulder County Flood Recovery." https://www.bouldercounty.org/disasters/flood/2013-flood.

Brennan, Charlie, and John Aguilar. "Eight Days, 1,000-Year Rain, 100-Year Flood." *Daily Camera*, September 21, 2013.

Broadhead, Wade. "History of Pueblo." Pueblo.org, 2014. Accessed September 2016. http://pueblo.org/history.

Bronson, Caitlin. "America's Top Ten Disaster Prone States." Insurance Business America, November 5, 2014. http://www.insurancebusinessmag.com.

Burt, Christopher C. "The Great Colorado Flood of May 30–31, 1935: One of the State's Top Three?" WunderBlog. Weather Underground, September 18, 2013. Accessed September 2016. https://www.wunderground.com.

*Cherry Creek Flood 1933* (film). Western History & Genealogy Department. Denver Public Library. Accessed December 10, 2016. https://www.youtube.com/watch?v=OiaGxj10qq0.

City of Pueblo. "The Great Flood of 1921." Document Center. Accessed October 2016. https://www.pueblo.us.

Clark, Champ. *Flood*. Planet Earth. Alexandria, VA: Time Life Books, 1982.

# Bibliography

Colorado Division of Homeland Security & Emergency Management. "Historical Colorado Flood Events." Department of Public Safety. Accessed August 2016. http://www.coemergency.com/2010/03.

*Colorado Experience: The Big Thompson Flood.* Rocky Mountain PBS. History of Colorado State Historical Fund. Aired October 6, 2016.

"Colorado Remembers the Big Thompson Canyon Flash Flood of 1976." NOAA News. National Oceanic Atmospheric Association. Accessed September 2016. http://www.noaanews.noaa.gov.

*Colorado Springs Business Journal.* "Incoming Tide." April 26, 2013.

*Colorado Springs Gazette.* "Effects of the Storm." May 25, 1878.

———. "Many Lives Buildings Lost in Pueblo Flood." June 7, 1992.

Community Collaborative Rain, Hail and Snow Network. https://www.cocorahs.org.

Conway, W.F. "At Least 110 Meet Their Doom. Roll Call of Missing Shows that Number Answered the Death Call of the Flood at Eden—Graphic and Thrilling Stories by Gazette Staff Correspondents Who Hurried to the Scene. Score of Missing, Buried in the Sand, May Never Be Found." *Colorado Springs Gazette*, August 9, 1904.

*Daily Journal.* "2 Dead, 3 Missing in Denver Flood." July 15, 1912.

*Denver Post.* "How'd You Know?" May 9, 2009. Updated May 6, 2016.

Department of Homeland Security. "Floods." Accessed August 2016. https://www.ready.gov.

Dudley, Charles S. *Colorado Springs Gazette Telegraph.* April 10, 1962.

*Durango Wage Earner.* "What We Know About the Wreck." August 25, 1904.

Eisner, Burton. "Elbert Class of '35: Just Too Wet to Graduate." NOAA Website. Accessed February 2017. http://www.crh.noaa.gov.

Ellis, Jonathan. "Flood Memories and Threats Run Deep." *Canyon Courier*, August 4, 2004.

Erdmand, John. "Colorado Flash Flooding: How It Happened: How Unusual?" Severe Weather. The Weather Channel, October 16, 2013.

Erion, Doug. *The Big Thompson Disaster.* Big Thompson, CO: Big Thompson Canyon Flood Memorial, 2006.

Everhart, Gregory D. "Remembering the 1965 Arkansas River Flood in Southern Colorado." U.S. Army Corps of Engineers Albuquerque District, July 10, 2015.

Fennig, David. "2013–2015 United States Hail Loss Claims." National Insurance Crime Bureau, May 2, 2016.

"Flood Basics." Severe Weather 101: Floods. The National Severe Storms Laboratory. Accessed October 21, 2016. http://www.nssl.noaa.gov.

# Bibliography

"Flood Facts." *National Flood Insurance Program.* Federal Emergency Management Agency. Last updated September 27, 2016. Accessed September 30, 2016.

Fogelberg, Ben. "'Where Were You When the Dam Broke?': Castlewood Canyon Collects Flood of Memories." History Colorado. Originally published May 2002. Accessed September 2016. http://www.historycolorado.org.

Follansbee, Robert, and Edward E. Jones. *The Arkansas River Flood of June 2–5, 1921.* Washington, D.C.: Department of the Interior, 1922.

*Fort Collins Courier Colorado.* "Girls Drown in Cloudburst." June 3, 1921.

Groom, Kaelin M., and Casey D. Allen. "Denver's Forgotten Flood: The Geomorphologic Impacts of the 1933 Castlewood Dam Failure." *JOW* 53, no. 2 (spring 2014). Accessed February 2017. www.academia.edu.

*Herald Democrat.* "Denver Flood Sufferers Receive Needed Help." July 17, 1912.

*Herald Dispatch.* "Bear Creek Canyon, CO (other areas) Cloudburst Floods, July 1896." July 24, 1896.

Horan, Patty, et al. *The Night the Dam Gave Way: A Diary of Personal Accounts.* Franktown, CO: Castlewood Canyon State Park, 1997.

Hyde, Brian. "Flooding in Park Hill: Then and Now." *Greater Park Hill Community* (newspaper), August 1, 2015.

Iovine, Julie V. "A Tale of Two Main Streets: The Towns that Inspired Disney Are Searching for a Little Magic of Their Own." *New York Times,* October 15, 1998.

Lucaciu, Loli. "Colorado Hail Storm Delivers Tennis Ball–Size Ice." CNN, July 29, 2016. Accessed February, 2017. http://www.cnn.com.

Lynn, Katie Keller, Sid Covington, et al. "Rocky Mountain National Park Geologic Resource Evaluation Report." National Park Service Geologic Resources Division, 2004. Accessed February 2016. http://www.wikimedia.com.

Massengill, Pat. "Centennial Race Track." Littleton, Colorado, January 2004. Accessed September 2016. https://www.littletongov.org.

———. "The 1965 Flood of the South Platte River." Littleton, Colorado, January 2004. Accessed January 2017. https://www.littletongov.org.

McGhee, Tom. "Colorado's Flood History Led to Changes." *Denver Post,* September 19, 2013.

Nash, Jay Robert. *Darkest Hours.* New York: M. Evans & Company, 1976.

National Oceanic Atmospheric Administration. "This Month in Climate History: June 3, 1921." Colorado Flooding National Centers for

Environmental Information. Accessed September 2016. https://www.ncdc.noaa.gov.
National Oceanic Atmospheric Association. "Weather Fatalities." Accessed August 10, 2016. http://www.nws.noaa.gov/om/hazstats.shtml.
National Park Service. "Front Range Floods Teacher Guide." Rocky Mountain National Park. Washington, D.C.: U.S. Department of Interior, n.d. https://www.nps.gov.
National Weather Service. "Denver Flood History Chronology by Year." Urban Drainage and Flood Control District. http://udfcd.org/flood-safety. Accessed September 2016.
Nelson, Mike. *Colorado Weather Almanac*. Boulder, CO: Johnson Books, 2007.
———. *The Colorado Weather Book*. Englewood, CO: Westcliffe Publishers, 1999.
Nelson, Sarah M. *Denver: An Archeological History*. Philadelphia: University of Pennsylvania Press, 2009.
Nystrom, Lynn A. "Amy Pruden Receives Grant to Study Recent Colorado Flood Effects on Antibiotic Resistance." Virginia Tech News, January 21, 2014. Accessed January 2017. https://www.eng.vt.edu.
Officer Down Memorial Page. "Officer Michael Owen Conley." Accessed January 2017. https://www.odmp.org.
———. "Sergeant Willis Hugh Purdy." Accessed January 2017. http://www.odmp.org.
Philipps, Dave. "Natural Disasters: A Repeat of Dreaded Flood Is Springs' Biggest Threat." *Colorado Springs Gazette*, May 27, 2011. http://gazette.com.
Redd, Nola Taylor. "Flood Facts, Type of Flooding, Floods in History." Live Science, October 11, 2012. Accessed September 2016. http://www.livescience.com.
*Rifle Reveille*. "A Terrible Flood: More than Twenty-Five Drowned." July 31, 1896.
Rudolph, Katie. "August 3, 1933: Castlewood Dam Breaks, Floods Denver." Western History & Genealogy Department. Denver Public Library website. Accessed December 2016. https://history.denverlibrary.org.
*Sacramento Daily Union*. "Aftermath of the Colorado Cloudburst." July 26, 1896.
Sherier, J.M. "Climatological Data. Colorado Section." U.S. Department of Agriculture, Weather Bureau, May 1935. Accessed August 2016. https://pubs.usgs.gov/pp/1019/report.pdf.

# Bibliography

Southern Colorado History. "The 1921 Pueblo Flood." Accessed September 2016. http://www.southerncoloradohistory.wikispaces.com.

*St. Petersburg Evening Independent.* "Estes Park, CO Dam Collapse and Flood, July 1982." July 16, 1982.

Strescino, Peter. "Floods Inundate Denver." *Pueblo Chieftain*, July 14, 1912. https://groups.google.com/forum/#!topic/arkriver/MSFre9o5Ung.

Telecommunications History Group, Inc. "The 1921 Pueblo Flood." Disasters. Virtual Museum. Accessed September 2016. http://www.telcomhistory.org/vm/disastersPueblo.shtml.

*Time.* "Top Ten Historic U.S. Floods." Accessed December 2016. http://content.time.com.

Town of Jamestown. "Jamestown 2013 Flood Facts." Accessed January 2013. https://sites.google.com/a/jamestownco.org.

Urban Drainage and Flood Control District. "Bear Creek Drainage Basin"; "Flood History." Accessed November 2016. http://www.udfcd.org.

U.S. Geological Survey. "1976: Big Thompson Flood Colorado 30 Years Later." Washington, D.C.: U.S. Department of the Interior, July 2006. https://pubs.usgs.gov.

U.S. Geological Survey and National Oceanic Atmospheric Administration. "Storm and Flood, of July 31–August 1, 1976, in the Big Thompson River and Cache la Poudre River Basins, Larimer and Weld Counties, Colorado." Washington, D.C.: U.S. Government Printing Office, 1979. http://www.bigthompson.co.

Vickers, William B. *History of the City of Denver, Arapahoe County, Colorado, Containing a History of the State of Colorado, from its earliest settlement to the present time, embracing its geographical, physical and climatic features, its agricultural, stock-growing, railroad and mining interests &c; a condensed sketch of Arapahoe County, a history of the City of Denver, giving an account of its early settlement and growth, its improvements, its business and industries, churches, schools &c; Biographical Sketches, Portraits of Some of the Early Settlers and Prominent Men; Views of Public Buildings, Private Residences, Business Houses &c, &c,.* Chicago: O.L. Baskin & Co., Historical Publishers, 1880. https://archive.org/details/historyofcityofd00inolba.

Webley, Kayla. "Big Thompson Canyon, Colorado, 1976." "Top Ten Historic U.S. Floods." *Time*, May 11, 2011. Accessed August 2016. http://www.time.com.

Wharton, Junius E. *History of the City of Denver: From Its Earliest Settlement to the Present Time to Which is Added a Full and Complete Business Directory of the City.* Denver, CO: Byers & Dailey, Printers, 1866.

## Bibliography

Wheeler, Keith. *The Chroniclers*. The Old West. Fairfax, VA: Time Life Books, 1976.

———. *The Townsmen*. The Old West. Fairfax, VA: Time Life Books, 1975.

Yore, Clement. "Estes Park Region Was Formerly the Playground of the Arapaho Indians," *Estes Park Trail*, January 27, 1922, 7, and February 3, 1922, 7–8.

# ABOUT THE AUTHOR

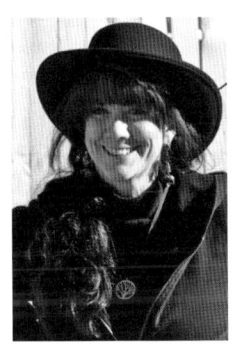

Darla Sue Dollman, BA, MFA, spent her life in areas prone to flooding, from the mountains and plains of Colorado to the Hill Country of Texas. She worked as a photojournalist for thirty-eight years covering weather disasters for local and national news sources, magazines and websites.

Dollman used her meticulous attention to detail working both as a legal and private investigator. She served on the English department faculty at Colorado State University and taught at other Colorado colleges and universities, as well. She now volunteers with the National Weather Service as a storm spotter in Weld County, Colorado. She writes about weather disasters on her Wild West Weather website and about Colorado history on her Wild West History blog.

*Visit us at*
www.historypress.net

*This title is also available as an e-book*